"To be an artist is to struggle; that's what it's about. We who make music bring beauty and blessing to the planet."
Judy Collins, p. 49

Contents

ON THE COVER

For the cover of our "Foremothers" issue, we had the idea that it would be nice to show an image of a quilt. Not only because quilting is traditionally a woman's art, but as a metaphor it captures how the stories of these women, woven together, create a more remarkable image that tells an even bigger story. So we got in touch with Caitlin Cary, who we knew was working with textile art, to fashion us a sort of quilt-like image. We chose Elizabeth Cotten because her story is the oldest in this issue, and it doesn't get more "Foremothery" than that.

Inside covers:
Lyrics from Hazel & Alice's "Don't Put Her Down, You Helped Put Her There." Illustrations by Drew Christie.

NO DEPRESSION TEAM
Chris Wadsworth *Publisher*
Kim Ruehl *Editor-in-Chief*
Stacy Chandler *Assistant Editor*
Brittney McKenna *News & Social Media Editor*
Sonja Nelson *Advertising*
Henry Carrigan *Print Partnerships*
Maureen Cross *Finance/Operations*

WEB nodepression.com
TWITTER & INSTAGRAM @nodepression
FACEBOOK facebook.com/nodepressionmag

GENERAL INQUIRIES
info@nodepression.com

ONLINE ADVERTISING
advertising@nodepression.com

SUBSCRIPTIONS
nodepression.com/subscribe

JOURNAL DESIGN & PRODUCTION
Marcus Amaker

Printed in Canada by Hemlock Printers, 100% carbon neutral

No Depression is part of the FreshGrass Foundation.
freshgrass.org
ISBN-10:0-9973317-6-3
ISBN-13:978-0-9973317-6-9
©2017, FreshGrass, LLC

Hello Stranger

BY KIM RUEHL

One night in my youth — I don't recall the exact circumstances, but I was definitely younger than 21 — I went out to a field with a cluster of friends and strangers just to look up at the stars. By that time,  granted, the night sky was no stranger to me. The starry night has been a friend since childhood, when it was the first thing I sought on camping trips. In college, I gobbled up stories of ancient Greeks and Romans, who sought their gods and goddesses in the sky, imagining pictures of men and beasts by connecting the dots of shining stars. To look at stars is to gaze back in time — the light we see from Orion's belt beamed out into the darkness years ago, and will only just reach our eyes tonight.

But this particular night, we were looking for the Pleiades. Beyond Orion sits a dark patch of sky with a cloudy light about it. Shift your eyes ever-so-slightly and that cloud of light becomes a cluster of about 250 young stars, though most folks can only see six to ten of them. Where Orion (the hunter) is the past, those dimmer stars, known as the Seven Sisters, are the future. That the ancient Greeks saw these new stars as elusive and dim too, should tell us something about our place in the universe. Thousands of years later, those 250 stars — taking up a tiny patch of the vast sky — have yet to realize their full light. The parade of human history that has gazed upon them has been, to them,
like a mosquito buzzing by at dusk.

This scene surfaced in my mind as I made the 90-minute drive from my home in Asheville, North Carolina, to the Carter Family Fold in Southwest Virginia, for a story you can find on page 22. I was thinking about how so much of what we know about American roots music is through the lens of men. The tendency of music writers to tell the stories of women in relation to their men has always struck me as ... unfortunate. Yet I too have been asked by editors to qualify phrases like "singer-songwriter" with the word "female," as though "male" is the baseline of normal, and anything outside of that must be explained.

We tell the stories of our music stars as though they are warriors and bulls and gods we've immortalized. But when we consider the "sisters," we tend to start with the men behind whom they stood.

The Carters we know through the story of their patriarch, AP, who went into the hills to collect hundreds of songs. But the story of that family band also exists through the eyes of Sara and Maybelle, who raised six children between them, sewed clothes, canned vegetables, struggled in marriages, moved around the country, and still somehow managed to turn the country music establishment upside down.

Elizabeth Cotten we know because Pete Seeger brought her on his television
show and Mike Seeger recorded her. But by the time she met the Seegers and, somewhat accidentally, became "discovered" by them, she was decades into adulthood. Her story stands apart from the ways they recorded her music. It seemed to me time to consider Cotten's story as a standalone thing — a black woman like any black woman of her time, who paid the bills by serving white people, who raised her children and then raised their children and then helped raise even their children. Then, after all that, Cotten rode her brilliant guitar work and infectious songs into somewhat of a music career. That she wrote her first song at age 11 is notable, but what a life she led between that event and the one that saw the old woman in a recording studio laying it down to tape. We're told her story through the lens of the Seegers' discovery of her, but follow the light past Orion's belt on that one, and a universe of stories emerges.

When we decided to dedicate an entire issue of this magazine to these and other women, I had to get past the urge to throw up in my mouth a little bit, to avoid any avenue where people could call it our "Women's Issue." I was determined that this not be a collection of stories about girl bands and female singer-songwriters. Instead, I wanted us to shift our eyes just a little bit, see past the stars we're always gazing at, and look at these artists from a different angle. My hope was that this shift would open up galaxies of untold stories, and I reckon it did. I hope you enjoy them.

NO DEPRESSION

SHARP SHOOTER

SHARP SHOOTER

Annie Oakley lives on through the women of roots music

by Corbie Hill

"I think that every once in a while somebody comes along that is really just meant to shake everything up. People that were in that era at that time, that got to see [Oakley perform] and witness it firsthand, were really fucking lucky."

Sarah Shook

S **SINGER-SONGWRITER** Sarah Shook and her two sisters were raised to be good wives, mothers, and housekeepers — at least according to the version of Christianity to which her parents subscribed. But then, when she was eight or nine years old, Shook read a book about Annie Oakley. It was the kind of pocket biography that can be found in children's libraries, but there was enough in its pages to stoke young Shook's curiosity. The impression stuck: Annie Oakley, "Little Miss Sure Shot," was a superstar and an iconoclast, a woman who lived on her own terms. She had a talent — she could *shoot* — and she made that talent her life's pursuit rather than adhering to the traditional roles for women.

Shook says the book "planted the seed that you don't always have to live up to other people's expectations. Sometimes there are people out there whose lives take them down this different route, that the authoritative figures in their life didn't expect or didn't see coming, and probably wouldn't have approved of."

Shook certainly took a different path than the one her parents laid out for her: The girl who was raised in a fundamentalist Christian household in upstate New York, where secular music was forbidden, grew up to be a hard-edged country bandleader based in Chatham County, North Carolina, whose independent debut, *Sidelong,* was reissued on Bloodshot Records earlier this year. Now a mother herself, Shook is an atheist with a strong sense of social justice — and a taste for whiskey.

"You've been told your whole life [that] you exist for this reason — this is your job, this is your function," Shook says, speaking of Oakley but also of women in the modern music industry. "You find out, actually, I can do this other thing that nobody even mentioned should be on my radar because of my gender. And now here we are and I'm doing this. I'm at the top of the list, I'm at the head of the pack."

Whereas Shook is a songwriter and guitarist, Oakley was a phenomenal trick shot. And while there are obvious differences between their tools of choice, both are performers who oriented their lives on their own terms, bucking the conventional expectations of their gender, pursuing talents they discovered in themselves. It's that spirit that has made Oakley a touchstone for country women for generations.

Shaking Everything Up

Annie Oakley was born Phoebe Ann Mozee on August 13, 1860, in Darke County, Ohio. She was one of ten children, including a stillborn boy. She hated the name Phoebe, and dubbed herself Ann at a young age. She also insisted on the "Mozee" spelling, though many records spell the family name "Mosey." (At least two siblings later changed their last names to Moses.) The headstrong performer took a stage name after nearby Cincinnati's Oakley neighborhood.

Oakley was born into desperate poverty. At the age of eight, she shot her first gun (an apocryphal tale has her annoyed with a squirrel in the window

Sarah Shook

and shooting to make it leave), and soon enough she was surviving by it — hunting and selling her kills to the local grocer. Even as a child, Oakley was an exceptional shot. She was known for killing clean, wasting little meat.

As an adult, Oakley lived by the gun as a performer. For 17 seasons, she toured the world as one of the top-billed names on Buffalo Bill's Wild West Show, shooting with precision, speed, and flair. She shot from horseback, sometimes standing in the saddle as her horse sped through the arena. In one trick, she somersaulted over a gun table, grabbing a rifle from it and blasting glass balls out of the air before she even landed. Oakley was a superstar who counted European royalty among her fans, who could and did shoot circles around even them, flouting protocol as it suited her.

"I think that every once in a while somebody comes along that is really just meant to shake everything up," Shook says. "People that were in that era at that time, that got to see [Oakley perform] and witness it firsthand, were really fucking lucky."

Despite her celebrity, though, Oakley remains a cryptic figure: Unlike her gregarious friend Buffalo Bill Cody, she guarded her privacy. She didn't say much to the press, and she kept her personal thoughts and life with husband Frank Butler to herself.

But audiences were hungry for her stories, and pulp novel after pulp novel, many cranked out during her lifetime, created a fantastical version of her. She's been the subject, too, of a heavily embellished 1935 biopic, as well as the musical *Annie Get Your Gun* and the 1950s TV show *Annie Oakley*. In the latter, a fictionalized version of Oakley lived in the Wild West town of Diablo, out-shooting ineffectual bandits in tidy half-hour episodes. However, beyond the polished version of Oakley that Hollywood proffered, there was the real woman of fantastic ability and resolve who owned the stage in her day.

"You'll look back to 1950s or '60s comics about Annie Oakley and she's portrayed as blond, which she was the opposite of," says Sophia Babb, who, along with her twin sister Joanna Grace Babb and violinist Nia Personette, plays in an Oklahoma City-based trio called Annie Oakley. "[There are] musicals about her and various shows that will include her in an episode as a character or some kind of trope."

"We have to explain a lot who she is — a surprising amount," Babb adds. "I thought she was just a known household name. I had heard her name all my life. I grew up in the country, around horses, [and] I knew who she was. A lot of people for some reason don't know who she is. ... A lot of times, people will ask, 'Which one of you is Annie?'"

The sisters, who turned 20 in August, have been playing melancholy roots music under the name Annie Oakley since their 16th summer. When the Babbs started performing, they didn't love the idea of billing themselves as Sophia and Grace. That just didn't have the right ring. They'd been on the lookout for a band name, and Sophia was a fan of the indie-rock band Miniature Tigers, who had a song called "Annie Oakley." The name lodged in her mind and it started showing up everywhere — in web comics, in TV documentaries — and Sophia got to Googling. The more she learned, the more fascinated she became.

She told her sister, "You know what? Let's just call the band Annie Oakley."

"She was this cool-ass lady," she adds. "We were just getting into feminism at that time, too, so I was like, 'What better way to represent our band than to pick Annie Oakley?'"

Granted, Oakley wasn't a traditional

Sophia Babb (left) and Grace Babb
are Annie Oakley the band.

feminist — notably, she had her doubts
about women's suffrage. But her persona
spoke to the Babb twins. She didn't trifle
with men who criticized her, and she
wasn't going to stop sharpshooting to be
more ladylike. What's more, she was
talented and confident and flourished
on her own terms.

Sound Techs, Not Sound Guys

Shooting was a men's sport in the 19th
century. Many shooting clubs didn't
allow women (though they'd make an
exception for Annie Oakley). While the
modern music industry isn't quite *that*
male-centric, the Babbs, like Sarah
Shook, identify with Oakley's life as a
female performer in a male-dominated
industry.

"While there are hundreds of
thousands of female musicians, in any
given music scene there are far more
men than women," explains Grace Babb.
"Being a woman in both the sharpshooting business and the music

industry — if you're good, you're kind of
a novelty in a way, and you have to keep
proving yourself."

Sophia adds that the inroads women
have made onstage in the music industry
are not matched on the business side,
where men still dominate.

"On the business side, there are so
few women," she says. "If you are an
artist, that's what you have to navigate to
become successful. There may be as
many women artists as we want, but if
the industry [side] is saturated only by
men, then women aren't represented in
the side that they most need to be
represented."

Shook has seen this, too. In a decade
of playing shows and working sound,
she's only seen one other female sound
tech. So she's taken the initiative, at
least within her band, to de-
masculinize the concept of a sound guy,
a door guy, a merch guy. When we talk,
she's just returned to her North
Carolina home from a Florida-and-
back tour with her band, the Disarmers.

Soon she'll return to her other job, at
longstanding Chapel Hill dive bar and
music room The Cave.

"As a woman who works in a music
venue, one of the things I've been doing
with my band right now, which has been
an interesting social experiment, [is]
I'm trying to retrain them to not call
sound techs 'sound guys,'" Shook says.
She's had to educate herself as well. "I've
always said 'sound guys.' Ever since I
started making music, that's the term
that you use.

"Then I start working at this music
venue. I get training, I learn how to run a
soundboard. I am, at this point in my
life, a sound tech."

It may seem like a small thing, but
consciously choosing to use the phrase
"sound tech" instead of "sound guy"
chips away at the idea that there are
men's roles and women's roles in the
music industry, with no crossover
between the two. Shook is glad that
publications like *She Shreds* exist to cover
women in the music industry, both

> ## "Being a woman in both the sharpshooting business and the music industry — if you're good, you're kind of a novelty in a way, and you have to keep proving yourself."
>
> Grace Babb (Annie Oakley)

performers and those with technical roles, but changing her own language and that of her bandmates helps them eliminate everyday preconceptions.

"Now when I say, 'Did we find the sound tech yet?' It changes what my expectations are," says Shook. "When we walk into a club, I'm not looking around for a guy to run sound for us. I'm looking around for the sound tech. Little tiny differences like that can make a huge difference in the long run."

Another thing about the music industry is a widespread expectation that musicians will hand off the business elements, and often to a man, says songwriter Arum Rae Valkonen, who blends indie-folk, neo-soul, and country blues when she takes the stage as Arum Rae. She splits her time between Manhattan and her family's farm in Virginia, and she holds a music business management degree from Berklee College of Music. Sure, she has a support team — manager, lawyer, agent — but she knows how to run her career.

We spoke a few days after the Los Angeles release show for her 2017 *Sub Rosa* release, during a tour with Sixto Rodriguez of *Searching for Sugar Man* fame. Aside from Rodriguez's daughter and granddaughter, who help run his business, Arum Rae is the only woman on this tour.

"[The men] can really help you out and I'm totally fine with somebody carrying my guitar and gear for me," Arum Rae says with a laugh. Then, in a more serious tone, she adds: "The old-

school thought of hiring a manager and looking for a man to give the okay still exists, and that is annoying. You have to learn how to assert yourself in a graceful way, because people want to look for you to be emotional or to be a bitch — all these things."

That's something Annie Oakley would appreciate, as she no doubt encountered the same during her tours. Indeed, Oakley hit the road just like a hard-touring musician. And in 17 years with Buffalo Bill's Wild West Show, she only ever missed four performances.

"As any touring actor or musician knows, touring takes its toll," writes Larry McMurtry in his book *The Colonel and Little Missie: Buffalo Bill, Annie Oakley, and the Beginnings of Superstardom in America.* "Annie and [her husband] Frank adapted to it better than [Buffalo Bill] Cody, whose tendency to burn the candle at both ends left him often irritable." In Oakley's case, contrary to stereotype, it wasn't a woman who wilted under the rigors of constant travel and hard work, but a man — and a tough guy, at that.

In her corner of the entertainment business and in her own era, Oakley evidently had little use for traditional roles or gender stereotypes. She met her husband Frank Butler, for instance, on the sharpshooter circuit; she out-shot him and they fell deeply in love. Throughout their life together he continued to perform, but she was the primary wage earner and he was the bookkeeper. When Oakley died in 1926,

Butler never ate again; he followed her in death 23 days later.

Additionally, Oakley believed in teaching women how to shoot, and often she did so for free. Like Shook, Arum Rae, and the Babb twins, Oakley knew there was no reason for men to dominate her field. She knew women could circumvent expectations and master any skill.

"It was surprising the number of supposedly 'idle' women who became capable of handling firearms," Oakley wrote in early 1920. "I have often been asked if women, as a class, can shoot a rifle or shotgun as well as men. My reply has been, 'Sex makes no difference.'"

'One Great Family'

An hour or so south of Chapel Hill, North Carolina, are the Sandhills, a rural region near the South Carolina border defined by sandy soils and longleaf pines. The area is rich with horse farms, too: acres upon acres of huge Southern ranches and conspicuous expanses of pastureland. In the early 20th century, this was where Wild West star Annie Oakley and her husband wintered.

As Dee Brown wrote in the intro of *Bury My Heart at Wounded Knee: An Indian History of the American West*, "Americans who have always looked westward when reading about this period should read this book facing eastward." Indeed, many of the people who helped create the 19th-century

American West as a folkloric ideal or a Homeric backdrop came from the developed East. Buckskin dresses and Wild West melodrama were Oakley's work. But to relax, she sought the nascent North Carolina resort town of Pinehurst.

In 1895, when a 35-year-old Oakley was already a decade into heavy touring with Buffalo Bill's Wild West, a moneyed Massachusetts businessman bought several thousand acres in the Sandhills. James Walker Tufts quickly built a resort village on his land, choosing the "Pinehurst" moniker from a list of rejected names for Martha's Vineyard. And, since much of the native forest had been clear-cut by a railroad company, Tufts planted pines.

In 2017, Pinehurst remains a resort village with huge houses, meticulously manicured yards and public areas, and a renowned golf course. Its median household income, per the US Census Bureau's 2011-2015 American Community Survey's five-year estimates, is $74,849, versus $46,868 for the state of North Carolina. The town is also overwhelmingly white — as of the 2010 census, it was 92.8 percent white, versus 72.4 percent for the state that same year.

Many of Pinehurst's residents retired from wealth or prominence. This has always been the nature of the town; when superstar Annie Oakley wintered here, her vacationing contemporaries included the Sousas and the Rockefellers.

In the village's private library, the Tufts Archives catalogs Pinehurst's 122-year history. Its Annie Oakley exhibit includes photos, shotgun shells, clay pigeons, powder tins, a double-barreled shotgun, and a rifle. Yet without Oakley alive to wield it, to make it sing, the long, well-worn rifle in the display case is, honestly, just a gun. Taken alone, it doesn't tell you anything about the woman, no matter how long you look at it. Then again, as Shook noted, the

people who got to see Oakley perform in person were the lucky ones. We are left only with relics under glass and newspaper reports.

"If you have the nerve to stand up to it, she might shoot an apple off the top of your head or shoot the ashes off the tip of your cigarette," an excited columnist for the village paper gushed in March 1920.

"Without practice or preparation, she commenced a bit of close rifle work in the neighborhood of Frank Butler and her setter Dave that spoke a world of confidence," read a separate *Pinehurst Outlook* story from three years earlier, when Oakley was 56. It praised her sheer skill: her speed, accuracy, and aura of effortlessness. "She broke a ball [that was being] whirled around a man's head on the end of a string while she was looking the other way into the blade of a table knife to get the direction."

The archive's Annie Oakley box contains a number of folders full of century-old news clippings and even some of Butler's original correspondence, yellowed with time. The couple never owned a place in Pinehurst, but they stayed either at the monumental Carolina Hotel or in an apartment in the "Thistle Cottage," which is now a single-family dwelling.

In late 1916 and early 1917, the sharpshooter's first winter in the area, the *Pinehurst Outlook* published its "Memories of Annie Oakley" column. It was written by a columnist who reported on conversations with her, which is likely one reason the columns present her unguarded self. "Memories" was a society column. If Oakley's life on the road came up in conversation, the unattributed columnist would report what Oakley said.

As she recalled from earlier in her career (it's important to note that Oakley never completely retired — not even during her leisure time in Pinehurst), she toured with a diverse crowd in the Wild West Show. If it was

unusual in the 19th century that a woman should be world famous for her acrobatic gunplay, it was just as rare that Cody would hire Native Americans to play themselves. Yet he hired a lot of them.

"I travelled with [Cody] for seventeen years," Oakley recalled to the "Memories" columnist. "There were thousands of men in that outfit during that time, Comanches and cowboys and Cossacks and Arabs and every kind of person. And the whole time we were one great family."

This camaraderie didn't always translate in the Wild West performances themselves, though. Sitting Bull walked into the arena to boos and catcalls for the "Killer of Custer," Brown wrote in *Bury My Heart at Wounded Knee*, but also drew sizable crowds. Afterward, these same hecklers descended on Sitting Bull in droves to buy autographed photos.

Black Elk, an Oglala who toured with the Wild West Show when he was in his early 20s, told John G. Neihardt for the book *Black Elk Speaks,* "I liked the part of the show we made, but not the part the Wasichus [white people] made."

Indeed, the showbiz side of the Wild West Show included indigenous dances, and also dramatized battles and shootouts in which the natives "died," night after night. Only recently had these indigenous performers survived the bloody conclusion of the actual Indian Wars firsthand. They had witnessed the slaughter of their people — real deaths that had been quickly translated into mass entertainment. Yet Cody, a fair and uncommonly generous showrunner, earned Black Elk's respect. "He had a strong heart," Black Elk recalled decades later.

Anti-Native prejudice peppered the language of the "Memories" columnist, but not Oakley's recollections. She offhandedly noted after a fox hunt that she was Sioux, having been adopted into the tribe by her close friend Sitting Bull, gently scandalizing her posh contemporaries. But then she described the person she'd known — intelligent, resilient, and taciturn with most Wasichus, but happy to share the story of his life with Oakley in "a kind of reserved and halting *Iliad* covering half a century." He called her Mochin ChillaWyntonys Cecilia, which translates as, "My daughter, Little Sure Shot." Diminutives like this didn't escape Oakley's notice. Queen Victoria once called her "a very clever little girl," though Oakley pointed out she was a grown, married woman at the time.

Nonetheless, their close friendship meant Oakley bitterly lamented Sitting Bull's murder, even 26 years after the fact, which the *Pinehurst Outlook* columnist gleefully printed in the paper's social pages.

Fact and Fiction

Bland Simpson has been a member of lighthearted North Carolina folk fusion band Red Clay Ramblers since the mid-1980s. In 1991, he and his frequent songwriting collaborator Jim Wann wrote "Annie Oakley," which appeared on their album *Rambler*. Simpson lives in Chapel Hill, and admits he became fascinated when he learned about Oakley's North Carolina connection.

As a kid, he saw the 1950s *Annie Oakley* TV show, which portrayed Oakley as a peppy girl-next-door who inevitably had to shoot a coin out of someone's hand or blow six holes in a tin can before it hit the ground.

"I sort of remember her running in the intro frames with a big smile ... today [she would] have been called cute. Pigtails and 16 or 17 years old, like a Mouseketeer," Simpson says. It didn't seem historical, really, and it didn't get into the real Annie Oakley's life as a hard-touring performer.

Even as he grew and learned more, Simpson still thought of Oakley in way-out-west terms, someone he associated more with Colorado or Wyoming than the wooded, developed East. But when he learned she was a sometime-North Carolinian, he felt compelled to write about her. He looked into what the real Annie Oakley did in Pinehurst, such as teaching women to shoot, but didn't find anything dramatic enough to hang a song on. So he and Wann made something up.

"We figured out the romance, somebody in the stands she'd had a relationship with, which was a fiction because it was Frank for her and that was it," Simpson explains. "When we wrote it, we thought, that'll be something true, at least for the person in the song."

Yet "Annie Oakley" evolved in Simpson's understanding the more he performed the song. He gradually realized it was about a delusional fan, not an ex-lover. The narrator is a fanatic; he's just another guy in the grandstands who imagines that he's had this relationship with a living legend, that he taught her everything she knows, and then when she rides by on horseback she'll recognize him among the thousands and he'll be elevated from the audience.

"This guy has never spent a second with Annie Oakley," Simpson says, his tone registering either pity or contempt.

Thinking back, Simpson's not even sure Oakley has an analogue today. Sure, in her day there were acts touring the Vaudeville circuit, and those would be late 19th- and early 20th-century equivalents of most of today's touring musicians. But if you look at small-town papers from those days, Simpson suggests, it's likely you won't have heard of the Vaudeville or variety show acts who were on the road. These were small-scale or even midlevel entertainers, like most of today's musicians, versus the Wild West Show's train full of performers, equipment, entourage, horses, and bison. Even a U2 or Rolling Stones tour is an indirect parallel, as the Wild West Show was basically a bustling village on wheels. Cody, like PT Barnum, helped invent the touring megashow. It simply hadn't been done before.

"They just didn't have rivals," says Simpson. "They didn't have 40 or 60 or 80 rivals the way a top music act now would have dozens of other top music acts that could go out and play the same circuit. At that level, where you needed a massive train, I think that was the biggest of the big time."

Indeed, Cody and Oakley dominated the market, and both names echo in our modern myth of the Wild West. As such, both have become legends in the realm of country and western music and culture. Both have a reputation for being badasses, according to fellow badass Sarah Shook. Shook suggests that Cody is better known than Oakley because the sharpshooter was hesitant to share her thoughts and feelings with the general public.

"I think," says Shook, "that human beings have a tendency, when we don't have all the facts, [to] fill in the blanks with whatever makes sense to us through the lens of our own personal experience."

To that end, Sophia Babb has a theory: "I think she wanted to compensate for having this vagabond lifestyle, for being a sharpshooter on a horse — and [for being] a woman. She wanted to be very conservative in all the other parts that she could." And maybe she's right. Maybe that's why Annie Oakley survives as a folkloric character as much as an historical one, the archetypal Western woman, and why she continues to inspire women entertainers nine decades after her death. With varying levels of success and accuracy, historians, screenwriters, and musicians have tried to fill in the gaps in Oakley's story, the things she felt no need to explain.

As for Oakley, she let her talent do the talking. ∎

HER OWN STORY, HER OWN SOUL

Big Mama Thornton lived the blues

by Lee Zimmerman

BY THE TIME OF HER death in 1984, Big Mama Thornton had broken numerous barriers for women performers by being a fearless, singular force in the blues world. Her booming vocals and impressive skills on the blues harp influenced definitive vocalists like Janis Joplin and Janiva Magness and have been rediscovered in recent years as a new generation of singers has found inspiration through the defiant precedent she set.

But the road she took was never easy. Two of her most enduring accomplishments — being the first artist to record the song "Hound Dog," three years before Elvis Presley turned it into a worldwide rock-and-roll staple, and writing the song "Ball 'n' Chain," which later became closely identified with Joplin — still left her fighting for recognition.

In the 1940s and '50s, when black Americans were overtly marginalized through Jim Crow laws, she made her presence known beyond the black community, through sheer talent and tenacity. She did it even while refusing to play by the rules or conform to artistic expectations. Later in her life, she challenged society's ideas about gender by dressing like a man and singing songs full of sexual innuendo, something that struck many people as shocking then and often still does today.

Larger than life, both in size and in style, she acquired her nickname when she first took the stage at the storied Apollo Theater. It was there that theater manager Frank Schiffman dubbed her "Big Mama." But by that time, she had long since learned how to wield her commanding presence as both a woman and a singer.

Loud and Proud

Willie Mae Thornton was born in Ariton, Alabama, in 1926. Her father was a Baptist minister, and her mother was a singer, and both instilled in her a love for gospel music. It was natural, then, that she sang in the church choir along with her six siblings. But soon her trajectory veered toward the less expected: life as a big-voiced, openly gay, frequently cross-dressing blues singer.

Thornton had her share of challenges early on. As a teenager, she was over six feet tall, leading to frequent ridicule from her peers. Her mother died when Thornton was barely in her teens, so she had to leave school at the age of 14 and work in a local bar, where she did thankless tasks like cleaning the spittoons. Her growing awareness of blues music set her off in pursuit of a music career, and she was eventually discovered either during a talent contest or while filling in for a singer in the bar where she worked. Historians don't seem to agree which event was the catalyst for her career, but they do agree she was given her first gig with an Atlanta-based troupe called the Hot Harlem Revue. With that group, Thornton found an opportunity to pursue her craft and develop her own style. She taught herself to play harmonica and drums by imitating others, and she pulled from her personal experiences when she sang, enveloping each song in raw emotion. The way she tackled songs was often crude and suggestive, and her heavy drinking often made her performances brash and belligerent, but Thornton's style set a precedent for any number of iconic artists who would follow years later.

"Big Mama Thornton's style was not drawn from traditional female archetypes," says blues educator, singer, and harmonicist Doug Harris. "If you expected dainty ... she was anything but. Big Mama sang about real life with power and feeling, and unabashedly expressed her sexuality in a way that was not typical for her time. Though capable of singing pretty and understated, her voice was loud and proud."

Eleanor Whitmore, who plays in Steve Earle's band when she's not performing as one-half of The Mastersons, was especially drawn to Big Mama Thornton's influence. "If you aren't moved by the power of Big Mama Thornton's voice, you probably don't have a pulse," she says. "She forged her own way in a largely male-dominated industry by being a multi-instrumentalist, writing her own songs, playing on sexuality, dressing like a man, all in addition to the force she was vocally. She was honest and authentic and had the whole package, which is what all of us hope to aspire to as artists."

Of course Thornton had her role models, too — blues singers like Bessie Smith, Ma Rainey, and Memphis Minnie, among others. Their individuality, particularly the way they conveyed their feelings and opinions through powerful, gritty renditions of early blues standards, paved the way for Thornton's strikingly singular delivery. Because they had already broken some barriers, Thornton was free to skirt polite pretense, coming straight to the point, enticing her listeners with overt sexuality.

"When I was comin' up, listening to Bessie Smith and all, they sung from their heart and soul and expressed themselves," Thornton told *The New York Times* in 1980. "That's why when I do a song by Jimmy Reed or somebody, I have my own way of singing it. ... I want to be me. I like to put myself into whatever I'm doing so I can feel it."

That arresting individuality remains a big part of her appeal to artists working today. "She was no bullshit, period," says blues singer-songwriter Delbert McClinton. "She was just real. Real can be upsetting. It can be uplifting, but above all it gets your attention. And she got everybody's attention in a most sensuous, primitive way. Her music let everybody get loose. It demanded that you get loose! Her life would have scared the shit out of most people."

'Some Real-Ass Blues'

Thornton's big break came when she moved to Houston, Texas, in 1948. The timing seemed ideal. The juke joints were booming, and the music that scene fostered was propelled by a sass and swing that allowed her to express herself with an obvious boldness and bravado. It also gave her opportunity to mingle with, and learn from, other important artists of that era.

"When she wound up in Houston, there was a lot going on there," says Texas-based blues singer Marcia Ball. "Lightning Hopkins was there. Bobby Bland was there, along with all that stuff that was coming out of the juke joints. She found her own way and stayed long enough to make some records."

Singer Trudy Lynn, who covers Thornton's song "All Right Baby" on her latest LP, *I'll Sing the Blues for You*, recalls seeing her in Houston early on. "Although I never had the chance to meet Big Mama, I would catch glances of her," Lynn recalls. "I was prone to sneaking around the club scene when I was a kid. There were a bunch of clubs in Houston's Fifth Ward where the black performers would play, such as Whispering Pines, Hamilton Inn, and the famous Club Matinee on Lyons Avenue. Club Matinee stayed open all night, serving food along with the live music. The black artists would all stay in the hotel, which was situated atop Club Matinee. The owner even had his own cab company running out of the same location. This was a real juke joint."

Thornton's brassy personality didn't jive with the respectable demeanor most women performers put across at the time. She flaunted her unorthodox personality with sexually charged material and an onstage presence that was often improvised, insurgent, and over-the-top.

"She forged her own way in a largely male-dominated industry by being a multi-instrumentalist, writing her own songs, playing on sexuality, dressing like a man, all in addition to the force she was vocally. She was honest and authentic and had the whole package, which is what all of us hope to aspire to as artists."

Eleanor Whitmore (The Mastersons)

"What's most profound to me about Big Mama Thornton is not only the raw power of her voice, but the confidence that it took for her to sing with so much certainty," says blues singer Bonnie Bishop. "She was a spitfire. Oftentimes, it is the lesser-known artists who end up making the deepest impact, because they influence so many other artists and singers, generation after generation. [She] is one of those artists. You can put on her records 50 years after they were recorded and the ballsy-ness of it knocks you out, track after track. There's no disguising that voice, [there's] nothing flowery about the recordings. It's just a real woman singing some real-ass blues."

The Original 'Hound Dog'

Following her stint in Houston, Thornton was lured to Los Angeles by bandleader Johnny Otis to appear in a revue that also included artists such as Little Esther and Mel Walker. Otis also helped her land a contract with Peacock Records in 1951, and it was for Peacock that she recorded around 30 songs, including "Hound Dog," which had been written specifically for her by the songwriting team of Jerry Leiber and Mike Stoller.

Thornton's "Hound Dog" was released

in 1953 and went to number one on the R&B charts, making its singer a star, one of the few women to attain such stature at the time. Yet the record was also plagued by controversy. Otis claimed that, as the record's producer, he was entitled to share in the songwriting credits. Thornton herself insisted that she improvised some of the lyrics and enhanced the arrangements with her exaggerated vocal inflections, and was therefore also entitled to a songwriter credit. To add insult to injury, Elvis Presley recorded the song three years later, scoring a huge mainstream hit with it and effectively relegating Big Mama's recording to the status of a rock-and-roll history footnote. She claimed she received a single check in the amount of $500 in lieu of the credit she deserved for putting her stamp on the song.

Though Elvis got more credit than she did for "Hound Dog," musicians continue to discover the original source. "I was 13 or 14 years old and I didn't have a lot of records, but I had Big Mama Thornton's 'Hound Dog,'" Delbert McClinton remembers. "I took my copy of the record with me to a party, but I never saw it since. Over the years I've come to figure that at least somebody else recognized how important it was and just had to have it."

Regardless of the contention around it, with her version of "Hound Dog," Thornton's career was already on the climb. She had made her first appearance at the Apollo one year earlier, in 1952, and later traveled the R&B circuit with bigger stars like Junior Parker, Johnny Ace, Esther Phillips, and Clarence Gatemouth Brown. In 1956, she resettled in Los Angeles, only to find that mainstream interest in the blues had begun to wane. She lost her deal with Peacock but continued to perform and eventually landed in San Francisco.

As the 1960s began, music fans developed a renewed interest in the blues, and Thornton was able to ride that wave, resuscitating her career in the process. She played the Monterey Jazz Festival in 1964 and 1966, toured Europe with the American Folk Blues Festival, and subsequently signed with Arhoolie Records, which has also championed artists like Elizabeth Cotten, Charlie Musselwhite, Rebirth Brass Band, and others. Thornton recorded three albums for the label during that decade — *In Europe, Big Mama Thornton with the Muddy Waters Blues Band,* and *Ball 'n' Chain.*

"Big Mama Thornton's recordings really stood out for me," says Grammy-

> "You can put on her records 50 years after they were recorded and the ballsy-ness of it knocks you out, track after track. There's no disguising that voice, [there's] nothing flowery about the recordings. It's just a real woman singing some real-ass blues."
>
> Bonnie Bishop

nominated blues artist Janiva Magness. "It was clear from the very first note that this woman had no issue with her power or control. She was in total charge of her voice, stage, and self. And she wrote songs — hit songs!"

She did so during an era when the national music scene was packed with a number of blues giants — among them, Buddy Guy, Eddie Boyd, Walter Horton, Fred McDowell, Sammy Strayhorn, James Cotton, Otis Spann, and Muddy Walters. Much of the reputation Thornton gained during this time was on her own accord, but it was Janis Joplin's recording of "Ball 'n' Chain" that helped bring her further forward for white audiences. Joplin's version of the song was a highlight of her breakthrough album with Big Brother and the Holding Company, *Cheap Thrills,* and Joplin's performance of the song at the 1967 Monterey Pop Festival made her an immediate star. Thornton was said to have remarked at the time, "That girl feels like I do."

Thornton's version of "Ball 'n' Chain," meanwhile, got lost in the mix. White audiences who perhaps didn't know better learned the song from Joplin's version, having no idea that it was originally recorded — iconically — by Thornton. Joplin, who first heard

Thornton sing the song at a bar in San Francisco, tried to correct that by frequently citing Thornton as an influence and arranging to have her open at several concerts.

"The money didn't go behind Big Mama Thornton," says McClinton. "Nobody developed her as something special. I guess it would have been very difficult to do because [her music] was so primitive. But she was also beautiful. She could move you. It's not something that should have been a hard sell.

"Her vocal interpretations were so primitive," he clarifies. "By 'primitive' I mean this feeling that's been around for ten million years. That's what she expressed. It was a voice that was a million years old. She was a mighty force. Someone who was letting out so [much] emotion. There was no avoiding that."

Despite the fact that she didn't have the big-money support that artists like Joplin and Presley received, Thornton appeared regularly at clubs and festivals throughout the '60s and '70s. In 1972, she rejoined the American Folk Blues Festival for an extensive European tour. She found some of her greatest success when she signed with Mercury Records in 1969 and released *Stronger Than Dirt,* her best-

selling effort and one that finally broke her on the pop charts when it reached number 198 on the Billboard Top 200. However, it was *Saved,* the gospel album she recorded for the Pentagram label in 1973, that her biographers note gave her the greatest satisfaction. It allowed her to fulfill a longstanding desire to return to her gospel roots via standards like "Oh, Happy Day," "Down by the Riverside," "Glory, Glory Hallelujah," and "Swing Low, Sweet Chariot."

As the '70s gave way to the '80s, Thornton took part in several major festivals as well as making television appearances on *The Dick Cavett Show* and a PBS special, *Three Generations of Blues.* Nominated for the Blues Music Awards six times, she was inducted into the Blues Foundation Hall of Fame in 1984.

A Lingering Legacy

In her later years, Thornton's reputation for brassy performances and heavy drinking was well established. Her penchant for dressing in men's attire — often wearing work clothes or occasionally donning a three-piece suit — cast a spotlight on her sexuality and singled her out at a time when most LGBT people necessarily remained closeted.

"I [heard] from a friend who actually played bass in her band that she was tough as nails," Magness relates. "I mean, the whole band was afraid of her in a way that more than demanded respect. He told a tale of her not liking what the drummer was playing and that he had given her lip before the show. So, right about mid-tune, she turned around and cold-cocked him. Punched him in the face. And with one blow, [she] knocked him out, clean off the bandstand! Then she kept the band playing without the drummer the rest of the night. That's a true story. Nobody was tougher at a time when women were not allowed to be boss. She was the boss."

As author Michael Spörke points out in his authoritative book, *Big Mama Thornton: The Life and Music,* the fact that she was six feet tall and weighed over 300 pounds didn't exactly encourage anyone to defy her.

Roots music publicist Cary Baker is still in awe of the performance he once witnessed. "My second-ever rock concert," he recalls, "and my first without parental supervision, was Albert King and Big Mama Thornton at Chicago's short-lived Kinetic Playground — a psychedelic dungeon fashioned after the Fillmore, with strobes, gels, light shows, and opium dens. I was 12 years old and had seen the photo of Big Mama on the cover of her album, which portrayed her in the visual tradition of classic blues singers Bessie Smith, Victoria Spivey, and Ma Rainey. So imagine my surprise when a much-slimmed Big Mama, donning a work shirt and pants, took the stage. Her singing melted the crowd, and I, for one, never appreciated her harmonica prowess until that night."

Unfortunately, years of hard drinking began taking their toll. Even though she continued to perform in her final years, her weight dropped dramatically, from 350 pounds to a near-skeletal 95.

"I played with her one time at Fitzgerald's in Chicago," Marcia Ball recalls. "It was a year before she died. She was small. ... She certainly wasn't 'Big Mama,' not that scary presence anymore. I met her that night and she was drinking gin and milk because her stomach was real messed up at the time. The story was that she had ulcers, but since she was still going to drink, she'd have some milk with it too. It was late in her career, but there was still that amazing presence. I was very aware of the fact that I was in the company of a pioneer, the genuine article, a woman who had forged the way for people like me."

On July 25, 1984, Thornton was found dead on the houseboat in San Francisco where she had been living. The cause of death was heart and liver disease attributed to alcohol abuse. She was 57 years old.

"Eventually, self-medication and health and the ravages of time began to do what an entire society's disapproval or disinterest could not, but her fire kept burning to the very end," says rock singer Cait Brennan. "When she died, *The New York Times* called her an 'aggressive blues shouter.' I think they intended it as a compliment, but the subtext is pretty clear. Real pain, real joy may come out as 'aggressive' or 'shouting' when you're used to a sort of stultifying, suffocating gentility. That's not life, at least not the life I've lived, and certainly not the life Willie Mae lived. She felt it all and lived it all without apology.

"She sang because she had to," Brennan adds. "In her, I don't see someone who was trying to intentionally transgress any unwritten rules of gender or sexuality or race or economics or anything else. I just see someone who was absolutely unable to be anybody but herself. All anyone has is their own authentic story and their own soul. I'm grateful she shared hers with us." ∎

ALWAYS ON THE SUNNY SIDE

A short history of American music through the women of the Carter Family

by Kim Ruehl

> "Grandma [Maybelle] loved the music and loved the fans and loved making people forget about their worries for a few minutes by playing live. Then so did Helen, Anita, and [June]. They were really driven by being these young, thirsty-for-more girls who loved this music with all their hearts, and were so proud to be out there representing it."
>
> Carlene Carter

NINETY YEARS AGO, ON THE border of Tennessee and Virginia — in a town so small and charming, both states claim part of it as their own — three people walked through a door for a music audition. They were a young woman named Sara; her husband, Alvin Pleasant ("AP"); and her teenaged cousin Maybelle. The whole thing was AP's idea, though it's not like he had to twist the women's arms. They had been making music together since AP and Sara married, and Maybelle married AP's brother Ezra. They performed in churches and at small community events and sang together quite a bit at home. Though it has occasionally been referred to as such, the audition wasn't exactly a lark, since its executive, Ralph Peer, had been corresponding with AP throughout the summer. Still, earlier that day, as the trio got ready to make the 25-mile drive from their rural mountain hamlet of Maces Spring, Virginia, to the bustling town of Bristol, Maybelle wondered aloud if she should bring her guitar.

Only with about a century of hindsight does this scene seem both silly and monumental. Those two women and that man, going under the plain, direct name of the Carter Family, came to reorient the music industry with their interpretations of old folk songs, providing an indelible link between music that has since become perceived as populist and progressive (folk) and music that is historically conservative (country). That these two seemingly disparate branches of American music came off the same family tree — via one deeply rooted family — itself suggests a well of stories.

Among them: how a young woman who was so seemingly unprepared for celebrity as to wonder if she should bring her guitar to a music audition would come to redefine how the instrument was played for generations of guitarists. And how, as though her own instrumental prowess and foundation-laying wasn't enough, she would come to put her own reputation on the line to introduce one of the other greatest guitarists of all time, Chet Atkins, to Music City a few decades later.

But walking through that door for the session, the Carters were just a man in overalls and a couple of "women from way back there," as Peer would later recall. "They looked like hillbillies."

Incidentally, during those same

sessions, a young railroad man named Jimmie Rodgers also showed up to record for Peer. Rodgers' charismatic personality and unmistakable yodel made him a hero to young boys everywhere, including Woody Guthrie, Hank Williams, Bob Dylan, and Johnny Cash. That fact is so widely known that the chain of music those men laid down is often considered the anchor of American roots music. Yet, among other sweeping influences that AP, Sara, Maybelle, and their long line of offspring would have over American music, it was a Carter Family melody that Guthrie chose for his most memorable anthem, "This Land Is Your Land," and it was a Carter girl named June who would pen one of Cash's biggest hit songs.

June's daughter Carlene is careful to point out: "You have to consider that 'Ring of Fire' is really a Carter Family song, because mom was very much a Carter Girl when she wrote that."

Into the Fold

About a half-hour northeast of Johnson City, Tennessee, US Highway 23 intersects with AP Carter Highway. Turn left and follow the curves through the mountains, past houses and churches, double-wide trailers and small family businesses, to where AP Carter Highway meets Wildwood Flower Lane. On your left is a large bare-wood structure that stretches up the hill behind it: The Carter Family Fold.

The structure, built in 1979, houses a performance space founded by AP and Sara's daughter Janette, a dance floor for cloggers, and bleacher seats that use the natural contours of the hill to provide views of the stage. Much like the family for whom its named, the Fold is more concerned about preserving the music of these ancient hills than it is about any of the trappings that come from the music industry at large.

Elsewhere on the property, which occupies about the equivalent of a single city block, sits AP's childhood home, the grocery store he ran until his death in 1960, a small stage he built behind his store and dubbed "The Park" for local musicians to perform, and a smattering of giant trees, flowers, picnic tables, and benches for enjoying the view.

The Fold is part venue, part museum, part living history exhibit, and a visitor wouldn't be mistaken in feeling like they're exploring somewhat of a monument. Placards tell the story of the Carters in brief, through the lens of AP's singular accomplishments as a song collector and patriarch. Quotes from family members (and one from country legend Marty Stuart) adorn the informational postings. Plaques commemorate the space as a state and national historical place. But as I

Carlene Carter

MARK HAUSER

Mother Maybelle in the studio with Nitty Gritty Dirt Band.

wandered there one summer morning, accompanied by a sweet old dog who seemed to come out of nowhere, I couldn't shake the feeling that the Fold was much more about AP than Maybelle and Sara. That it was there to preserve something AP, specifically, had handed down.

Indeed, the story of the Carters that's so often told is that through the lens of AP — a country man who collected some 300 songs in his life, no doubt a feat. Yet, in the scope of American folk and country music history, "Man walks into hills to collect songs" is not an unfamiliar story. Pete Seeger's father, Charles, collected songs, as did John and Alan Lomax and several others before and since. The impulse to explore America's nooks and crannies to find music worth recording pervaded a generation of a certain kind of man — and at least a couple women. But wandering the grounds of the Carter Family Fold, what intrigued me more were the stories of Maybelle and Sara — a couple of cousins who were strong, country women, who raised six children between them, canned fruit and pickled vegetables, sewed all their own clothes ("She was a seamstress ... she made her own bowling jacket," Maybelle's

grandson John Carter Cash told me), and somehow, above and beyond all that, also managed to turn the country music establishment on its head forever.

No monument has yet been erected in Maybelle and Sara's names, unless one considers the innumerable guitarists inspired by Maybelle's signature guitar method, the Carter Scratch, or the countless singers unashamed to sing out in their huskiest altos. And, in many ways, that's the story of women in American music — of women in America, in general: that preserving their legacy is more about maintaining oral history, celebrating what we've learned from them, while the men leave behind tangible structures to wander around. Neither of these things is more valid than the other, but the tangible structures give us a clear start to a story, whereas the legacies of women, so woven into the fabric of our culture, are more challenging to unravel from our own.

It's logical to wonder if, all things being equal, Sara and Maybelle would have entered the story of American music if not for AP's tireless collecting and pushing on the business side of their band. Singer-songwriter Rosanne Cash, who is not a Carter — though she

learned guitar under the tutelage of Maybelle's daughter Helen and spent a good deal of time with her stepmother June and others — struggles with that question as well. "It's really hard to pull those threads apart and know what would happen separately," she says. "It's like the Beatles: What would George and Ringo have done on their own without John and Paul? I don't know. But you do get the sense that Maybelle and Sara were more genuinely musical."

Cash's stepsister Carlene takes it a little further: "Had Grandma not left the valley with her little girls, [had she] and Aunt Sara not gone down to Del Rio, Texas, to try to keep the Carter Family going — and then Grandma bringing the girls to be on the Opry and stuff — that might not have carried on the way it did. That had a lot to do with the love my grandma had for playing the music.

"I think my Aunt Sara didn't really have the drive for it," she adds. "I think she definitely was a strong woman and strong-willed, and went about her way the way she wanted to, and [she] had that breathtakingly beautiful alto voice. But I think Grandma loved the music and loved the fans and loved making people forget about their worries for a few minutes by playing live. Then so did Helen, Anita, and mom. They were really driven by being these young, thirsty-for-more girls who loved this music with all their hearts, and were so proud to be out there representing it. Had they not done that, I don't know where we'd have been, honestly."

After a beat, she adds that the Carter Family legacy "was very driven by the women."

Guitar Hero

The story of how the Carters became a guiding light of a budding country music industry has been told time and again. But parts of it are well worth repeating.

Peer found in them a certain infectious authenticity, and they began recording in Bristol and New York. Obsessed with keeping their repertoire fresh, AP spent countless days, weeks, and months exploring Appalachia in search of other songs for them to sing. Back in Virginia, Sara fell in love with AP's cousin Coy, who moved to New Mexico and left Sara behind to divorce AP. Despite those severed ties, the band persisted.

They received a gig on the radio in Del Rio, Texas, where the station got around American signal limits by placing its tower over the border in Mexico. Like a number of other border radio — or "X" — stations, XERA had a signal so powerful it covered most of the United States; so powerful it's said that ranchmen could hear it in the wire of their cattle fences.

From Texas, Sara headed to New Mexico and then to California to marry Coy, sending her children back to Virginia with their father. Maybelle taught her daughters the songs AP had collected, moved to a small town in Missouri with Ezra and their family, and in 1950 landed in Nashvillle to start a run with the Grand Ole Opry.

When the Opry invited Maybelle & the Carter Sisters to appear, it was with the caveat that their guitarist, Chet Atkins, was not invited. To hear John Carter Cash tell it, this was because Atkins was so good, he intimidated the small community of Nashville guitarists, who were afraid he'd steal all their work. Maybelle refused to appear on the Opry without him, and eventually the powers that be relented.

"He took over the Grand Ole Opry stage," says John, "[and then] he took over Music Row in a matter of years, and developed the Nashville sound. If it hadn't been for Maybelle and the girls bringing their little guitar player, we wouldn't know country music as we do right now, just because Chet Atkins might not have ever been here."

By then, Maybelle was widely considered the matriarch of country music. She befriended a troupe of young hippies called the Nitty Gritty Dirt Band (she called them the Dirt Boys), who dedicated an entire album, *Will the Circle Be Unbroken*, to her and her family's songs. That album became foundational among folk, country, and Southern rock musicians, providing for those communities an education in American roots music akin to what Harry Smith's *Anthology of American Folk Music* had been for the folk revival. Following its influence over the decades, one would land smack in the lap of what's now called the Americana music industry.

"Maybelle Carter was among our first guitar heroes, for a lot of us," says Jeff Hanna, frontman of Nitty Gritty Dirt Band. "She was certainly mine. Being obsessed with folk music as a kid, learning to play 'Wildwood Flower' in that Carter fashion which we called the Carter Scratch ... [it was a] very beautiful, very inventive, resourceful way to play acoustic guitar.

"Years later, getting to actually play on a record with Maybelle ... and hanging with her in the studio was a dream come true. [She was an] amazing woman, had a beautiful presence — really sweet, angelic. She had a calming effect on us when we were making that *Circle* record, and we were super nervous being in the presence of all these giants like Earl Scruggs and Doc Watson and Merle Travis and Roy Acuff. But she'd walk into that studio every day just chilled out, cleaned up our language, and we'd just bask in her wonderfulness."

He pauses and then adds the same thing most people add when talking about Maybelle and the Carters: "The impact of the Carter Family has been a great thing in all of our lives."

But for all that little family band would affect in the music industry, they would go right on being the people they were back in Maces Spring. For Carlene Carter, they were just the elders.

"[Maybelle] was my absolute favorite person," she says. "I cried to go to Grandma's, I cried when I had to leave Grandma's. She was my best pal ever. She taught me how to play guitar. She put an autoharp in my arms before I ever knew [it]. ... She made me coffee when she was playing cards with Minnie Snow, who was her best pal and they played canasta and poker. I'd be up there with the gals playing cards when I was just a little kid. I didn't know what I was doing, but I thought I was *in*."

Later, she adds, "They were really down-to-earth people, considering the esteem people hold them in now. Grandma was very happy — she had a Cadillac and enough money to go gamble every once in a while on the slot machines, or just to go play bingo. ... She always put out a big garden and cans. [That] was just part of her life that she carried back from Virginia, from the valley where she lived. She brought it to Nashville with her and it never changed. They put out this huge garden every year, her and granddaddy, and she'd be out there working her tail off, making jam and every once in a while she'd make some plum wine."

The Carters hailed from the isolated hills, where everyone was poor and separated from the mainstream. As is

"If it hadn't been for Maybelle and the girls bringing their little guitar player, we wouldn't know country music as we do right now, just because Chet Atkins might not have ever been here."

John Carter Cash

true of much of Appalachian culture from that time, communities supported one another regardless of age, sex, and race. While white folks in the cities were holding fast to Jim Crow laws and keeping women from the workplace, everyone in the mountains had to do their part — and everyone did. Though disparity existed, it wasn't at all ironic for poor white Christian country musicians to be proud of their strong women, learn from their black neighbors, look to their God and elders for guidance, and make whiskey in the bathtub to share with everyone from the preacher to the sheriff.

"We come from bootleggers," Carlene says with a laugh. "Moonshine makers."

As for race relations, on his song collecting trips, AP was frequently accompanied by a black guitarist named Lesley Riddle. Riddle, it would turn out, was regarded more fondly within the family than its own patriarch — as late as the mid-'60s, Maybelle was on the record gushing about Riddle's great skills and spirit.

Riddle taught his two-finger method of guitar playing to Maybelle, who used it on occasion and introduced it to others. Though she always gave him credit, this was one instance among many across American music history where some method of black music-making was appropriated by white players, only to draw greater attention for the white player. Whereas other musicians who borrowed from black players simply appropriated methods and moved on, Maybelle Carter shared Riddle's name whenever she played guitar like he did.

In the '60s, inspired by Maybelle's adoration of Riddle, who had long since moved on from pursuing music in any

way, Mike Seeger tracked him down in Rochester, New York, and recorded a collection of his songs for Rounder Records — just one of many ways the Carters brought forward the music of Appalachia into the wider musical vernacular.

Carrying Culture

Listening to the Carter Family in 2017, you can still hear the elements that endeared the trio to audiences a half-century ago. Sara's arresting, otherworldly alto voice feels more like something she's channeling than something her vocal cords do. Home in on the guitar parts and you must remind yourself that's just one woman playing one instrument. There's no flash or pizazz to the harmonies or production, but none is needed.

Imagine hearing this over the radio waves in a city like Chicago or Little Rock, or a town the size of Macon, Georgia, long before television or national news was so accessible. You would have no personal experience of those hills, but the music would have shown them to you. It would have struck you as the heartsong of universal human hope and pain, an offering of the idea that humans ultimately face the same questions and cares no matter how separate they feel from one another. Put more plainly: The Carter Family was music personified.

Few understand this as thoroughly as Rosanne Cash, who straddles two deeply rooted lines of consequential families in American music. She is not directly related to the Carters, though she became part of their wider family culture when her father, Johnny, married into the clan via June Carter. It was June's sister Helen who taught a

young Rosanne to play the guitar, introducing the budding artist to music-making as a means of keeping a family legacy alive. The impression Helen made on Cash at the time, and that the Carters in general made as the years chugged along, planted in her memory what she recognizes as a "tremendous responsibility" to carry on the family culture in one way or another. "But it's not a burden responsibility," she adds. "It's a joy responsibility."

Likely because of her contact with the Carters, Cash's sense of duty to the family music line has proven to be a guiding force in her life as a musician, if not always in her career.

"I was in Dublin several years ago and I went in this antique store – an antique bookstore," she says. "There was this book on the shelf called *A History of Irish and Scottish Music*. It was this huge book, like six inches wide. So I pull it off of the shelf and it falls open in my hands to this page [that said,] 'John Cash, minstrel, 1840,' with a drawing of him. It looked like my family! It looked like a Cash. I got chills up my spine. It was like someone was saying, 'Keep it going. Keep it going, lassie.'"

Later, she adds, "I used to think when I was younger, 'Oh, this is just my dad, and it's such a heavy legacy and I just want to get away from it.' Then I got older and realized what a gift it was. It wasn't just my dad. I mean, his grandfather was the singing master in the church. And clearly going back into the depths of time there were Celtic musicians [in the family], because so much of that melancholy that's in my dad's music — and in mine as well — is deeply rooted in Celtic music. It's DNA stuff, it's not even thought out."

Indeed, much of the melancholy in her father's music was passed down in the bloodline — Johnny's mother sang to pass the time and ease her pain at the death of her oldest son, Jack, for example. But the hours Johnny Cash spent listening to the Carter Family on border radio from his farmhouse in Arkansas no doubt impressed upon him a certain allegiance to the potential for music to transcend one person's troubles, to speak on behalf of the universal human experience.

When Cash sang, "Get rhythm when you get the blues," he was echoing something he learned from Maybelle Carter before he ever shook her hand. In a sense, then, the music Rosanne had handed down to her came both directly and indirectly from the Carter Family — a fact she seems to recognize. "I have an ongoing and eternal debt that they taught me what they did," she says. "Those songs provided a foundation for so much."

The Family Business

"People say, 'Oh, I can play the Carter Scratch like your grandma.' I say, 'OK, do it.' So they do it and they're adding all these other notes, but they're missing all the nuances that she had, that nobody can figure out how to do," notes Carlene Carter, who turned to her family's legacy for 2014's *Carter Girl*. Spinning off that release, she plans to spend 2018 touring theaters and performing arts centers for a one-woman show, to deliver her takes on her family's legacy. As I would hear from John Carter Cash and his half-sister Rosanne, preserving the family's musical history is less "family business" and more an outgrowth of indebtedness. Some families pass down recipes; the Carters pass down songs.

And sure, the beauty of the Carter Family's extensive musical footprint, the

hundreds of songs for which AP is memorialized, is that their intrinsic universality makes them easy to learn. Anyone who knows the fundamentals of guitar playing can pick up a recording and pluck out the basic chord structure of "Wildwood Flower" or "Keep on the Sunny Side" or "No Depression in Heaven." But those who've built their careers on their family legacy each recognize that the versions they learned from Mother Maybelle were ever-so-slightly different from the recordings. While the recordings captured moments, the songs continued to grow from there. And that is where the life of music and the business of music — the folk and the country, respectively — diverge yet again. One is focused on getting people paychecks and the other is focused on, as Rosanne said, "Keep[ing] it going, lassie."

Indeed, the one thread I heard from Carlene, John, and Rosanne was that regardless of whether and how long the Carter Family's recordings continue to be printed, the family is committed to keeping the music going through their performances, and passing it down to children and grandchildren.

For Carlene, who has spent much of her career chasing her own voice and creative instincts, *Carter Girl* and the upcoming tour are somewhat of a homecoming, though she makes a point of noting that neither are much of a leap.

"Whenever I didn't know what to do, I always went back to the Carter Family music," she said. "It just soothes my soul and it fits my voice. I've always been kind of a rocker, a high-energy rocking country girl, and this stuff really feels good to me. I feel like I can bring ... an energy to it. I think that's what keeps it alive, is coming at it with a new energy

and a deep purpose about it."

When I ask her whether she feels an urgency to get younger generations of Carters into the fold, Carlene barely pauses to breathe. "I think that it's good for everyone to have a little bit more balance in their life before they partake in the career of being a Carter Girl," she says. "But I don't want [the Carter Family legacy] to die and I'm hoping that they embrace it at some point. They might just have a streak of me in them, where they want to do their own thing and find out who they are. Then they can come back to it and find a way to make it work for them, too."

To that end, Carlene's half-brother John alluded to a family-wide effort to keep some version of a Carter Family band going for the foreseeable future. Adding more links to the chain, he said, wouldn't just keep alive the songs, but also the spirit through which they were created.

"We're in the business of fun," he explains. "It's all about joy. It's about finding time to laugh onstage no matter where you are, because the music brings joy back to your heart. Music was therapy, it was solace, it was so much to my mother and my father. It was their very lifeblood, and at times, especially in my dad's last months of his life, music was his strength, his catharsis, his peace. ... He and my mother were the same way. Music, to my mom, was unadulterated joy and it was always there. She had a great work ethic that came from her mother and her father. Ezra of course managed Maybelle and the Carter Girls through the '40s. They always knew music and they always performed, and that was their life. From the moment she could walk until she shut her eyes for the final time, it was music." ∎

'IT'S NOT OVER YET!'

Roots music pioneer Alice Gerrard is still following the music

by Allison Hussey

I
N EARLY 2015, ALICE GERRARD stepped on stage at a small club in Durham, North Carolina, to join a benefit concert for NARAL Pro-Choice NC. She led a band of musicians half her age on her cheerful and encouraging "Get Up and Do Right." As the band tried to bring the song to a close, Gerrard rattled off a "two, three, four!" for one more round of the chorus. The musicians scrambled to keep up, but under Gerrard's direction, they brought the song to an exuberant finish. It was a fleeting but exemplary moment in Gerrard's music career: Even well into her 80s, she remains a youthful force who keeps everyone around her on their toes.

She's best known as one-half of the bluegrass duo Hazel and Alice, a band widely recognized as the first female-fronted bluegrass outfit, who helped pave the way for generations of young women to be leaders in bluegrass, old-time, and folk music. But Gerrard is far more than just a quick picker or a high, lonesome singer. To know her is also to know the profound depths to which her influence runs.

Gerrard was born on July 8, 1934, in Seattle, and grew up mostly in California. Her home was always full of music. Both of her parents (and many of their friends) were musicians, and Gerrard's mother toured in a family band called the Symphony Sisters Quartet. As a child, Gerrard took piano lessons at the behest of her parents but hated every minute of them — she wanted nothing to do with the rigid classical music they pushed.

She got hip to folk music while attending Ohio's Antioch College, fascinated by fellow students strumming guitars with no sheet music in sight. And, like many artists of her generation, she was captivated by Harry Smith's seminal *Anthology of American Folk Music*. Texas Gladden's "One Morning in May" was particularly alluring, and Gerrard felt drawn to Gladden's mournful, beguiling, unaccompanied voice. She taught herself to play guitar and some banjo, and eventually landed in Washington, DC, for work. Through friends of friends active in the music communities of Washington and Baltimore, Gerrard eventually met "this little girl with a great, big voice": Hazel Dickens.

Their partnership grew gradually, and didn't begin with the intention of it becoming a long-term recording project, Gerrard says. They frequently attended weekend parties where the main activity was casual, collaborative musicmaking. At some point, someone suggested that the two perform a song together.

"Hazel knew a zillion songs, and I was learning stuff, but I hadn't really sung very much in public or in front of people. We just started singing together," Gerrard says, adding that they never had their sights set on joining a band. They just wanted to play music together themselves, so they did.

For a time, there weren't many other women involved in their musical circles. "I was always very aware of the women who were playing this music, and was immediately drawn to other women. You could count them on one hand back in the '50s and early '60s," Gerrard says. Even so, those closest to Gerrard and Dickens — friends and fellow musicians alike — were thoroughly supportive of their efforts, and Gerrard says that she never felt as though she and Dickens were treated as novelties in a music scene where women were rare.

"We were surrounded by a very supportive community of my husband, [Dickens'] friends, the friends that she had become friends with in Baltimore," she says. "They wanted us to do what we did, and they were very encouraging of us."

Eventually, Hazel and Alice stepped into public view, beginning their careers as the first woman-fronted bluegrass group. They toured regularly, hopping into vans with the likes of Dock Boggs, Ola Belle Reed, Bessie Jones, and Roscoe Holcombe, making jaunts arranged by activist-musicians Anne Romaine and Bernice Johnson Reagon. These tours took them all over the South and beyond, allowing Gerrard and Dickens to spread

progressive, pro-labor, pro-equality messages in small, rural communities that might not have heard them otherwise. The two stayed active together through most of the '70s, releasing a few albums on Rounder Records. But after a few years, interpersonal tensions became too much to ignore.

After the &

"I feel in some ways like Hazel and I never successfully made a transition into equal partnerships. I was the mentee, and she was the mentor, and I was learning from her," Gerrard says. Though their working relationship played to each woman's strengths, any issues they had with each other often went unresolved. "We did talk about it to some extent, but nothing ever came of it. Our M.O. was just to kind of not deal with stuff."

The duo's partnership came to an end in the late '70s, not long after the release of their fifth album, *Hazel Dickens and Alice Gerrard,* on Rounder Records in 1976. The two pursued separate solo careers and interests, and Dickens passed away due to complications from pneumonia on April 22, 2011, at age 86.

Since their split, Gerrard has become a potent force on her own, dedicating her entire life to old-time music. She's always been a performer, but has also been one of the most active advocates and documentarians of the

music. She co-produced a 1983 documentary about Appalachian fiddler Tommy Jarrell, titled *Sprout Wings and Fly,* with Les Blank. In 1987, she founded *The Old-Time Herald,* a nonprofit magazine dedicated to nurturing and spreading the world about old-time music. It was the *Old-Time Herald,* in fact, that prompted her move from Galax, Virginia, to Durham, North Carolina, where she's lived for nearly 30 years. The city provided much better technical and logistical support for that operation than the rural Virginia hamlet could.

Gerrard's life's work is a treasure trove, some of which is housed at the University of North Carolina at Chapel Hill. In the Southern Folklife Collection at Wilson Library, there's an archive of materials from Gerrard that includes audio recordings, field notes, photographs, and more. Much of it has been digitized and can be examined for free online, but it would take even the most enthusiastic scholar weeks to sift through every piece.

A Teacher and a Learner

Gerrard is now 83, and she doesn't seem to have any intention of slowing down. She still plays regular gigs both around and outside Durham, with a rotating cast of collaborators. When she's home, she takes her dog, Polly, to nose-work

"I was always very aware of the women who were playing this music, and was immediately drawn to other women. You could count them on one hand back in the '50s and early '60s."

Alice Gerrard

and agility training classes. She remains an enthusiastic participant in progressive politics — she joined the Women's March on Washington last January and calls her local government representatives daily — and maintains an active online presence. She's working with a Durham-based filmmaker, Kenny Dalsheimer, on a documentary about her life and is also eyeing putting together a book of her photography from over the years.

Despite her accomplishments — including receiving a Lifetime Achievement Award from the International Bluegrass Music Association in 2001 — she's hesitant to claim recognition for herself. Fifty-plus years into her artistic career, she's still a little uneasy about any commendations.

"I'm honored by it, and I'm slightly mystified. Accepting, slightly uncomfortable," she says. She's also not keen on the occasional insinuation that her work is coming to an end.

"I know I did all that stuff, but there's also this element of, 'Well, it's not over yet!' Wait another ten years!" she says, a little exasperated.

But there are many who cheerfully, respectfully aren't holding their applause. Anna Roberts-Gevalt, who co-leads the bluegrass duo Anna & Elizabeth with Elizabeth LaPrelle, is among the youngest generation of musicians for whom Gerrard has been a guiding light. In college, she heard *Pioneering Women in Bluegrass*, a collection of Hazel & Alice songs compiled and released by Smithsonian Folkways in 1996. Roberts-Gevalt still cites it as a "hugely influential" record for her, and when it came time for her and LaPrelle to name their burgeoning music project, they knew they wanted to nod toward the two women who had inspired their journey.

LaPrelle and Roberts-Gevalt met Gerrard a few times through teaching at old-time music camps, and the two eventually recruited Gerrard to join them on a handful of songs on their first record, 2015's *Anna & Elizabeth*. Roberts-Gevalt says that they were so excited and nervous about asking Gerrard to work with them, they left a tittering message on her answering machine with their request.

"We called her up, and we left her this message on her answering machine being like, 'Heehee, Alice, will you be on our record?' " she says. They were delighted when Gerrard called them back.

"She was like, 'Hey, giggle girls! Of course I'll be on your record!' That was pretty rad and funny, and very Alice. She was just like, 'Duh, you guys, I don't know why this is a big deal.'"

Over the past few years, Roberts-Gevalt says she's formed a kinship with Gerrard over their shared journey to the music they both love. Roberts-Gevalt calls herself a "Yankee from New England" and says that, like Gerrard, her interests in old-time were a mix of musical and academic. Despite feeling like an interloper, she eventually became part of the fold.

"For me, Alice is a hero because she had a journey where she kind of fell in love with the music as an outsider. I kind of relate to that journey," she says. "The more I've gotten to know her, the more inspired I am by her journey in particular. I think any time you hear someone whose story is similar to your own, that's inspiring."

Gerrard — who remains a vivacious presence and player — continues to inspire people like Roberts-Gevalt through keeping up her work.

Roberts-Gevalt recalled a recent interview she did with Gerrard for *The Old-Time Herald* (which Gerrard no longer runs), part of a series where younger musicians interviewed older artists about their craft. Gerrard spoke with her at length about all the elders she'd learned from, and noted that they're all gone now.

"I was like, 'Well, Alice, you're our elder now.' She kind of said something like, 'Oh, shit!' It was kind of this, 'Oh, am I the elder now?' " Roberts-Gevalt recalls. "I love that about her, that she didn't think of herself as that. She's still a learner."

Gerrard still applies that active pursuit of learning to her work. It's a natural extension for her interest in many other strains of music, not just bluegrass.

> ## "The more I've gotten to know her, the more inspired I am by her journey in particular. I think any time you hear someone whose story is similar to your own, that's inspiring."
>
> Anna Roberts-Gevalt

"I'm kind of surprised at myself, actually. I'm very much a traditionalist at heart," she says. "I really love traditional sounds, and my love of bluegrass, for example, kind of ends with Bill Monroe and the Stanley Brothers. But at the same time, I really appreciate soul in music, wherever it comes from. I feel like I can recognize it if it's coming from France, or South America, or wherever. You can hear the soul in music that's real. That's kind of my only limit, I think.

"I like trying new things," she adds. "Especially when I feel like I can bring something to the table, and I do feel like I can, in most cases."

Following the Music

That interest in trying new things was a significant factor behind the development of Gerrard's fourth solo record, 2014's *Follow the Music.* The record came about after a few years of good-natured badgering from fellow Durham musician MC Taylor, who leads folk-rock band Hiss Golden Messenger. The two met through renowned bluegrass scholar Robert Cantwell while Taylor was earning his master's degree in folklore at UNC-Chapel Hill, and he ended up as her graduate teaching assistant in 2009 for a class she taught at the Center for Documentary Studies at Duke University. Taylor says he's loved Gerrard's music for many years. Even before he moved to North Carolina from California a decade ago, he knew that Gerrard was someone he wanted to meet.

"I was going to grad school and stuff, but one of my goals was that I was going to meet Alice Gerrard," he remembers. "I always thought that she was one of the deepest people making records on the old-time and bluegrass spectrum."

But it took a while for Gerrard to come around to Taylor's overtures. "I was like, '*What?* Why? Why me? What do you want?'" she says. "He did pester me, for quite a while. He talked about his vision for the album, and finally I said, 'Okay, why not?'"

Taylor served as the record's producer, and he called upon buddies of his who, for the most part, operated in rather different musical spheres from Gerrard to lend their talents to the album. That cast included brothers Phil and Brad Cook, two-thirds of the experimental folk-rock ensemble Megafaun, plus Town Mountain fiddler Bobby Britt and drummer Terry Lonergan. Gerrard jumped right in with the ensemble that Taylor rallied for the recording.

"I guess I had just decided to give myself up to it, to see what happens, and discovered in the process that these were such great musicians. Phil and Brad are just wonderful, I love playing with them," Gerrard says, adding, "I felt like it was a great experience. It opened my eyes to a whole other segment of music in this area and beyond."

Taylor, meanwhile, came to understand directly how Gerrard's "art-forward" approach to her work, as he puts it, gives her music timeless power.

"She's very adaptable as a musician, and she's very flexible as a person. She's super

wide-open, one of the most emotionally wide-open people I've ever met," he says.

Tompkins Square, a well-regarded independent record label, issued *Follow the Music* in September 2014. The LP nudged Gerrard back into a semi-national spotlight and even earned her a Grammy nomination for Best Folk Album. Though the trophy ultimately went to Old Crow Medicine Show for *Remedy,* there was still significant excitement surrounding the prospect that Gerrard might finally get the big-time recognition she deserved. She, meanwhile, wasn't fazed by all of the fanfare. In February 2015, shortly before she attended the awards ceremony in Los Angeles, she told Durham's *INDY Week,* "I don't really need a dryer; I can hang my clothes on the line, and I do. I don't really need a plaque to go on the wall. It's meaningful in the sense that it makes me feel good that my peers think that the work I've done is meaningful. Hazel grew to be much more accepting of the honors that she was given. I accept them, too, but I don't need them to live my life."

Gerrard already has what she needs: a loving family, a roof over her head. She's also got the enduring support from the communities she's bolstered over the decades. So what if she hasn't sold a million records? It's a fair bet that she's touched a million lives through her songs and influence. That's got to be better than a Grammy anyway. ∎

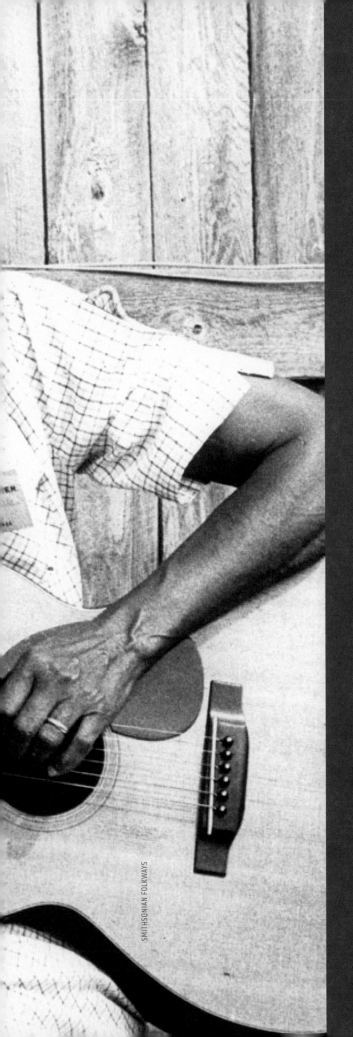

'BECAUSE I DON'T GIVE UP'

The 'accidents' that led Elizabeth Cotten to our ears

by Alexa Peters

realize there were always really good women guitar players," says John Miller, a guitarist and teacher who has transcribed much of Cotten's music for the instructional DVD *The Guitar of Elizabeth Cotten.* "I suspect that a lot of the really innovative and interesting women guitar players were socially relegated to possibly playing in church or playing in the kitchen, as opposed to becoming entertainers. Elizabeth Cotten's professional music career sort of happened by accident."

Indeed, it wouldn't be a stretch to say that "by accident" has always been Elizabeth Cotten's style. Nonetheless, she always cultivated the gifts she was given.

Her Brother's Banjo

"Every day at school they would call roll, and her teacher called her and she said, 'Sis, I know we call you "Sis" but do you have another name?' And Granny looked up and said, 'Yessum. Elizabeth,'" explains Cotten's great-granddaughter Brenda Evans. "She says she doesn't know where that name came from but she named herself Elizabeth because her parents didn't agree on a name for her."

Cotten was born in 1895, in Chapel Hill, North Carolina. Her mother, Louise Parks Nevilles, was a cook and her father, George Nevilles, a dynamite setter.

"My father was a *man*," Cotten told

EVER SINCE THE SEEGER family discovered her musical gift in the middle of the 20th century, Elizabeth Cotten has been a beacon for folk musicians. Her song "Freight Train" is the vehicle generations have used to travel into the rich worlds of folk and fingerstyle guitar. Still, for someone so vital in clearing a path for others, her own story exists in fragments, usually incorrect and out of time. It's to the extent that some actually thought Cotten was a myth, even after her music started reaching wider audiences in the 1950s.

In a sense, it's understandable that Cotten isn't a household name. She was a poor, black woman in the South in a time of blatant racial prejudice. Women of her era, let alone poor women of color, rarely had the luxury or access to become professional musicians. Plus, Cotten's late emergence wasn't predicated by an earlier recording career, like it was for Mississippi John Hurt and other of her peers who experienced a similar revitalization mid-century.

"I think it's important for people to

Mike Seeger in an interview for the 1968 Newport Folk Festival program guide. "He never wanted a easy job. If somebody offered him a easy job he'd say, 'Oh, that's a boy's job.' He wouldn't take it."

Cotten, the youngest of five children, took after her father's tenacious drive for self-definition. Her love of music began with her brother's homemade banjo, which she was discouraged from playing because she was left-handed. Regardless, Cotten would take it down and play it while her brother was at work, usually flipping it upside down, breaking a string and slinking off before he'd discovered what she did. As Cotten recounted between songs on her 1983 *Live!* album, he never scolded her, and that was encouragement enough.

Around the time her brother left home with his banjo, Cotten, then in the third grade, quit school and started working to buy her own guitar. In the 1967 Newport Folk Festival program, she told Seeger of getting hired to clean houses.

"I wasn't 12 years old," she said, "and I goes to work for this lady. Her name was Miss Ada Copeland. I'd give anything to find those people again. She paid me 75 cents a month. She said I was very smart."

Eventually, Cotten saved up enough to buy her first guitar, a $3.75 Stella. It was on that guitar that she wrote her iconic song "Freight Train" around age 11.

"I just loved to play," she told Seeger.

"That used to be all I'd do. I'd sit up late at night and play. My mama would say to me, 'Sis, put that thing down and go to bed.' 'Alright, Mama, just as soon as I finish — let me finish this.' Well, by me keepin' playing, you see, she'd go back to sleep and I'd sit up 30 minutes or longer than that after she'd tell me to stop playing. Sometimes I'd near play all night if she didn't wake up and tell me to go to bed."

By 1911, 16-year-old Cotten was married with a child, and gradually she drifted away from the guitar. If teenage motherhood wasn't enough, her church also dissuaded her from playing her "worldly" music, as Cotten notes on *Live!* When Pete Seeger asked her about this on his *Rainbow Quest* television show, she explained plainly: "When I joined the church, they told me not to play the ragtime songs and be a member of the church."

For the next three decades, she hardly touched the guitar. Cotten raised her daughter, Lily, and kept house until divorcing her husband in the early 1940s. She then moved to Washington, DC, where Lily was living, to help raise her grandchildren.

"She was very wise, and I think that she was before her time in many ways because, first of all, she got divorced," Evans said. "That's something that women then did not do."

Indeed, Cotten and Lily — whom the

children called Granny and Mama Lily, respectively — stayed in DC for many years, raising Cotten's grandchildren and great-grandchildren as two loving, headstrong matriarchs.

"When I talk about my great-grandmother I could go on forever because that's the impact she left on my life," said Evans. "When we were kids, she raised me as her daughter. Me, my brother, and my first cousin, she and her daughter, my grandma: We all lived in one big house and the kids had a great big bedroom at the front of the house. Imagine this — two double beds, a fold-up cart, a twin bed, and a kid on the floor. That's where we slept. And she slept in that room with us."

Evans, now 64, remembers her great-grandmother Elizabeth as her "angel on Earth."

"Granny always called me 'Sweetie Pie,'" she says. "And when I needed something sewn or made for a play she would hand-do it. She would get the thread and have me thread the needle and get the material, and from scratch she would make skirts — whatever I needed. She was caring, you know."

Everyone in the house, including Cotten, either went to school or worked. Then, around 1947, while Cotten was at one of her temporary jobs, she met the Seegers. She told the story on *Rainbow Quest:*

"When I came to Washington to live, ... I worked at Lansburgh department store. They gave me a job selling dolls. I was just there for the holidays. Thanksgiving, Christmas, and New Year's. Mrs. Seeger — Mike Seeger's mother, Pete's stepmother — walked in. She came in with two fine-looking children. That was Peggy and Barbara. She bought two dolls, one for each child. While she was waiting for the dolls to get wrapped, Peggy got lost in the store. I happened to be the one to find her and bring her in to her mother. Peggy was crying and I never could stand to see children cry, so when I brought her in the tears were coming down on my cheeks."

Grateful, and touched by Cotten's visible empathy, Ruth Seeger gave Cotten her telephone number in case she ever needed work. A month later, Cotten became the housekeeper for one of the most influential musical families of the 20th century. They were the first to call her "Libba," a nickname that would stick.

Music in the House

Ruth Crawford Seeger was a famed avant-garde composer and music teacher, and her husband, Charles Seeger, was one of the pioneers of modern-day ethnomusicology. Their children, especially Mike, Peggy, and Pete — Charles' already-prominent son from a previous marriage — also made significant contributions to American culture as musicians, activists, and folklorists. As a whole, the Seegers were instrumental in documenting and disseminating the traditional music of Appalachia and elsewhere for new generations of listeners who otherwise may not have been exposed to it. And,

because of Ruth and Charles' commitment to folk music — and Pete's — the Seeger household was an epicenter of folk music activity.

"Mike and Peggy would be sitting eating dinner and there'd be a knock on the door and it'd be Lead Belly or Woody Guthrie," says John Ullman, who, along with his wife, Irene Namkung, became Cotten's agent. "It was a pretty heavy environment."

As their housekeeper, Cotten was cooking while listening to the children's piano lessons, arranging the sheet music and *Hit Parade* magazines on the coffee table, and dusting around the five-string banjos and acoustic guitars. Naturally, she got to thinking about making music again.

"Peggy kept her guitar hanging in the kitchen. When Mrs. Seeger went and started teaching music, I would pick up Peggy's guitar and take it into the dining room and I'd close the doors so that I couldn't be heard," Cotten said on *Rainbow Quest.*

One day, while Cotten was playing "Freight Train" for herself, a teenaged Peggy and Mike Seeger overheard her. Dumbfounded, they begged Cotten to teach them her song, offering to dry dishes for her so they could listen to her play.

Eventually, the Seegers discovered she had more than just "Freight Train" in her repertoire, and Mike started to record the songs. Those early kitchen recordings gave Cotten the chance to perform in small living room shows for prominent people like senators James Abourezk and John F. Kennedy.

"When you love something, it never leaves you," explains Evans, recalling her great-grandma's return to music. "And by

the Seegers' playing and encouraging her, they took whatever reservations she had away from her. I think that the Seegers played a major role in terms of her being 'discovered.'"

By 1957, Mike Seeger had helped Cotten release her first album, *Elizabeth Cotten: Negro Folk Songs and Tunes,* reissued in 1989 as *Freight Train and Other North Carolina Folk Songs and Tunes* by Smithsonian Folkways. It's on that album that a 12-year-old Evans sings "Shake Sugaree."

"Every night, after she finished her household chores, she would play and practice the guitar," says Evans. "Every night, she would play and I would think, 'How does she make the guitar sound like this?' It was remarkable how she played. That's how 'Shake Sugaree' came about. We were little kids, and she said, 'You all listen to this tune, help me write some words to this melody.' All of us kids had verses in that particular song."

Until her death, Cotten often called Evans to come out and sing with her, because she knew how much Evans loved to sing. The pair had many colorful experiences while touring — namely at the Newport Folk Festival and the Smithsonian Folk Festival — where Evans had the chance to meet luminaries like B.B. King and Joan Baez.

"I used to beg to sing," recalls Evans. "I love music and I love all genres of music, and Granny exposed me to a type of music that I probably would not have been exposed to if not for her — folk music. Back then, the Supremes and Temptations were just coming up. I didn't know anything about folk music. Black youth didn't listen to folk music."

Indeed, the folk revival was primarily

a phenomenon of the white American youth, as was much of the later counterculture revolution. It was the white bohemians who learned Lead Belly's "Goodnight Irene" in the quads of their college campuses and wore out their recordings of The Weavers.

As editors Ajay Heble and Rob Wallace wrote in their book, *People Get Ready*, "White musicians were learning to play and sing in the styles of both white and black folk musicians, yet at the same time, many older black musicians were having their careers rejuvenated by the revival, and the styles of music they played were being exposed to people who had long

forgotten them or had never heard them in the first place."

Learning and Teaching

Ullman and Namkung were among this young group obsessed with the rediscovery of traditional songs. They went to Reed College in Portland, Oregon, which had a concert series that brought to campus traditional artists like Reverend Gary Davis and others. "The people I was around [at Reed] said if you're serious about getting into folk music, learn 'Freight Train,'" Ullman recalls. "That's sort of the model song for fingerstyle

guitar. So, I started trying to learn that. Then people told me, 'Go see this guy Barry Hansen and he'll lend you whatever records that you want.'"

As Ullman and Namkung fanned the flames of their obsession, kindled by Cotten's music, they started booking acts at Reed. Eventually, they began the Seattle Folklore Society with friends Phil and Vivian Williams in the mid-1960s. To this day, the society works to preserve and support folk music in the Pacific Northwest.

"We started putting on concerts," Ullman says, "but the significant thing is that we wanted to have these people

"I don't think she's taught [to guitar students] as much as she should be. I think it's partially because people think her music is so much simpler than it is. It's subtle and it's sort of high-concept, a lot of it. It's not simple conceptually. But I think because it's not really flashy, people don't appreciate how complex what she's doing was."

John Miller

around and learn from them. It wasn't so much that we were performing a public service as we were following our desires to learn this stuff."

In 1968, Mike Seeger brought Cotten on tour in the Pacific Northwest with his band New Lost City Ramblers. That gave Ullman the chance not only to book Cotten, but also host her at his house and get to know her personally.

"We had Libba on tour maybe four or five times a year, and two or three of those times she might stop through Portland and stay at our house," says Ullman. "She really liked turkey — roast turkey. She basically said, I can't make that for myself anymore, so we'd make it for her. Then she would make chicken and dumplings for us. That was her go-to dish.

"One night," he recalls, "I got up and walked into the kitchen and Elizabeth was sitting at the kitchen table and she'd gotten the [leftover] turkey out and she'd made herself a turkey sandwich that was three or four inches thick. She had the sandwich halfway between the plate and her mouth. She looks at me and she says, 'John, you know, some old people don't have an appetite. But me, I've got an appetite. And you know why? Because I don't give up.'"

Ullman and Namkung became

Cotten's official agents in the early '70s, as she toured in promotion of *Freight Train and Other North Carolina Folk Songs*, and her second release, *Shake Sugaree, Volume Two*, which Smithsonian Folkways released in 1967.

It was at a pair of 1969 shows that Ullman and Namkung booked, at Bellevue Community College and Seattle's University Friends Meeting House, that Flip Breskin first heard and fell in love with Elizabeth Cotten's music. Breskin, along with Ullman and Namkung, are among some of the only people outside of Cotten's family that got to spend quality time with her during the height of her career. As a consequence, they have unique insight into who Cotten was and are full of unheard memories of Cotten that go beyond her often-told vignettes. Both elucidate, too, the important role Cotten played for many in the Pacific Northwest, where she often toured.

Breskin was enrolled in a music theory class at Bellevue Community College when she was asked to introduce their special guest, Libba Cotten, for a show in the lunchroom later that day. "People were playing pool, eating, talking, rattling dishes. They were not there to hear Libba. ... I listened and was not particularly moved or interested,"

Breskin said.

A couple of nights later, Breskin went to see Cotten again at the University Friends Meeting House, the Quaker facility near University of Washington.

"Quakers are into listening and that space was set up for it. Everybody was there to listen. And, something happened out of that chemistry — there was support for Libba to pour her whole heart and soul into what she was playing. And, at some point, while sitting out there in the audience, my heart filled up and then poured over into tears. And I sat there shaking with tears rolling down my cheeks and came out of that concert thinking, 'I could do that and that's worth doing.' I think it was a key pivot point for my whole life."

Breskin has since spent her life deeply committed to learning music and encouraging others to do the same. Aside from being a noteworthy concert promoter, teacher, and folk musician herself, Breskin was instrumental in starting Puget Sound Guitar Workshop, a summer music retreat grounded in sharing and learning songs from a diverse community of musicians. The camp has been an incredibly impactful for a large community of musicians in the Pacific Northwest and beyond, but without

Cotten, Breskin isn't sure it would've happened.

In 1971, Breskin and Cotten met again when Breskin booked the coffee house at Western Washington University and brought Cotten to play. Breskin ended up hosting Cotten for dinner that night, and from then on the two were close. Breskin fondly refers to the legend as her "guitar grandma." The learning gift Cotten gave Breskin inspired Breskin to offer that same gift to others.

"We hung out, meaning we would [play guitar] and she would let me learn her stuff. Her process was to sit and play the same tune up to speed all the way through for a couple hours straight while I hung on to her coattails and tried to figure out what she was doing. She was extraordinarily patient."

Always Recognize

Cotten, who personified dignity, wasn't the type, even in jest, to boast about her newfound popularity. She was humble and always strived to see the humanity in others.

"She didn't change at all [after she became known]. She did not change not one single bit," said Evans. "She respected everybody. I never seen her disrespect anyone. Our household was one that if a homeless person walked down the street, ... two women who didn't know them would have them come in and have a meal. I raised my kids that way. ... You can determine which way or how to do so, but always recognize people. She taught me that."

What people found so welcoming about Cotten's music, and the progenitors of the traditional styles in general, was that their songs and performances were so consistently raw, idiosyncratic, and human, the antithesis of much of the hyper-produced music of the day.

"What I had [before hearing Libba] was the people who had learned from the real stuff, who were one step removed and far smoother. It had been cleaned up so that the singing was all on pitch, there weren't extra beats to measures, and it had been Europeanized. Bob Dylan was the only one who didn't sing 'pretty,' and there was a way he was very reassuring to me that someone could sing and not have to be [perfect]," Breskin said. "Then I heard Libba," she adds, clarifying that Cotten was one of the first non-commercial folksingers she'd ever met, and the impression she left ran deep.

Beyond her raw, human approach to the music, Cotten defied the standards of the day in the way she played — flipping a right-handed guitar upside down, thereby changing the way the strings lay on the fretboard. The lowest pitched string, often used for bass notes, lay by her index finger, and the high-pitched strings used for melody lay by her thumb. This gave her melody a fatter, warmer sound and her bass a finer, sharper bounce. This is opposite of how a guitar is played by the typical right-handed player, and was wholly unique to Cotten.

"When I was transcribing her," explains John Miller, "because she played left handed and upside down, I'd be watching her and I'd be saying to myself, 'What's she doing with the bass?' I'd be watching her picking thumb and realize that she was using her thumb to play the melody and her index finger to play the bass. So, even after I knew [what] the method of her [guitar] playing was, I still had to remind myself constantly that she's not using her picking hand as I'm accustomed to it being used."

Though self-taught, Cotten had an active imagination and an ear for contrapuntal movement — a nuanced musical technique. This gave her songs intricate interior lines within the chords, like you might hear sung by the alto and

tenor voices in a choir. She put less emphasis on repetitive triads (chords built from the root note up in perfect thirds), than other songwriters typically did.

"I don't think she's taught [to guitar students] as much as she should be," says Miller. "I think it's partially because people think her music is so much simpler than it is. It's subtle and it's sort of high-concept, a lot of it. It's not simple conceptually. But I think because it's not really flashy, people don't appreciate how complex what she's doing was.

"For instance," he adds, " 'Freight Train' as she did it is just absolutely perfect. The melody is perfect, the interior voice leading is perfect, it's like all the choices are perfect. But as the song has been picked up and played by Nashville guitarists, they pretty much always change the melody in ways that are not improvements and, similarly with the voicing choices, the little interior movements tend to be lost."

While she was living, Cotten often noticed how her songs were misplayed, and though she never discouraged anyone, she did point out that fact. "I remember her commenting about how the white folks always do it wrong," says Breskin. "White people [came from the European tradition] and played the root. She never hit the root of the chord except at the very end of the song. She commented on [the variations] and noticed. For her to actually say something, it was a very big deal, but she could give you 'the look.' "

Despite that "look," Cotten was a generous and patient teacher. She was delighted when someone wanted to learn her music, and she would play for anyone who asked, for as long as they needed.

"She was giving me a huge gift of respecting me as a learner," says Breskin. "Having complete confidence that given the time, I could figure it out."

As she aged, Cotten's influence grew more profound. At 90, she became the oldest woman ever to win a Grammy, for *Elizabeth Cotten Live!* She continued to tour and perform solo and with performers like Hazel Dickens, Alice Gerrard, and Taj Mahal, all the way up until her death in 1987.

Even now, contemporary folk musicians are discovering Cotten and determining her story must continue to be told. Among those artists is Portland-based singer-songwriter Laura Veirs, who tells Cotten's story in a forthcoming children's book titled *Libba*.

"My parents sang 'Freight Train' to [get] me to sleep when I was a kid," says Veirs. "And then I learned her music when I became interested in country-blues guitar. What I liked about her story was ... she believed that people could accomplish anything at any age. That's a good message for children."

Indeed, Cotten had an undeniable effect on everyone with whom she came in contact. "Taj [Mahal], the Seegers, the Grateful Dead — all these people just took her as extremely important," notes Ullman. "From there, her music radiated out to other people."

'You Might Think about Looking'

One night in 1987, Ullman and Namkung were having a hard time sleeping. After a restless night, they were awakened at 5:30 a.m. by the ringing telephone. "I staggered into the office room and I picked up the phone and it was Jackie [Torrence]," says Ullman.

Torrence is a masterful storyteller, and another client Ullman and Namkung represented. About a year prior, Torrence and Cotten had bonded at a show that Ullman had booked for them. That was the only time the two women had met.

"Jackie said she'd just had this dream about Libba," Ullman recalls. "They were sitting on this porch in North Carolina, and Libba said, 'Don't the sun look pretty as it's setting in the evening?' And Jackie said, 'I don't see the sunset anymore, I'm so busy working and traveling.' And Libba says,

'You might think about looking.' "

As Torrence finished the account of her dream, the call waiting beeped on Ullman's phone. He switched it over to find Cotten's grandson, Larry Ellis, on the line. Cotten had just passed away at her home in Syracuse, New York.

Breskin spent that night sleepless, too, playing Cotten's songs with a friend. In a meticulously put-together photo book, Breskin still has several rarely seen photos of Cotten. One reveals Cotten's sweet, freckled face in a close-lipped smile, her eyes cast on Breskin, a soft hand wrapped around guitar frets. She is pensive, maternal, in her gaze.

"The depth of her musicality, and the apparent simplicity, opened the doors and inspired huge numbers of people," says Breskin. "Taj Mahal quoted that he wouldn't have gone where he went without her example as a left-handed guitarist. My generation, if you wanted to play fingerstyle guitar, the first tune most of us learned was 'Freight Train.' "

As it usually goes — particularly for poor women of color — Cotten's true legacy has only begun to crystallize now that she's gone. And it's extending beyond the professional musician and ethnomusicologist circles that originally revered her.

She lives on through listeners who never even liked folk music until they saw her pick the strings; through music hobbyists who shared, and continue to share, with friends in living rooms and around campfires; through the generations of children who were soothed to sleep by family renditions of "Freight Train." Perhaps Cotten's greatest legacy is seen through her great-granddaughter Brenda Evans, who still sings and now creates her own line of jewelry. Like so many others who have been touched by Elizabeth Cotten's life and music, Evans' unfazed pursuit of her passion, her gift for bringing others together through honest expression, mirrors that of her incomparably influential Granny Libba. ■

OUT LOUD

Judy Collins speaks her mind in song and society

by Henry Carrigan

AT THIS POINT IN AMERICAN MUSIC history, Judy Collins' songs and voice are pervasive. A fierce, strong woman who speaks her mind with boldness and candor, she reveals in her songs both the struggles and beauty of being an artist. Consider her take on Joni Mitchell's "Both Sides Now," Ian Tyson's "Someday Soon," Stephen Sondheim's "Send in the Clowns" — or her own compositions, like "My Father."

Alongside her talents, Collins' passions run deep: She's long supported artists and songwriters by singing their songs on her albums, often bringing notice to their work. She's devoted her own writing — in both songs and books — to topics close to her heart, such as her son's suicide and her relationships with food and the environment. She's long been committed to making the world a better place through her political and social activism. All of these things connect in her music as well, and we discussed all of this and more during a recent interview. It has been edited for continuity.

HENRY CARRIGAN: Let's start with your father. He was a huge influence on you. What are some of his most memorable traits?

JUDY COLLINS: He was just remarkable. Very gifted, smart, musical.

He played piano and sang. He was blind from the age of four. He went to a school for the deaf, dumb, and blind, and it had to have been a fantastic school. He carried his blindness off very well. He was intelligent, handsome, and charming. He was independent, funny, and talented.

My father was famous in Hollywood and in Denver. In Denver, he had a radio show on which he would read poetry and sing all the popular songs of the day, in his beautiful singing voice. My father was also an alcoholic. When he wasn't drinking, we had happy times, but when he was drinking, he was sad, and would often sob, and I could feel his pain.

My father was a great reader, and he read me books from the time I was born. His love of reading is a very powerful gift he gave me, and reading has been a lifelong obsession of mine.

HC: What about your mother? What are her most memorable traits?

JC: She was a graceful and very accomplished woman. She was able to raise five children, and that alone is an accomplishment.

My mother also had a gift of music — she played

> **"Leonard Cohen came to my house, and he sang me 'Suzanne.' I loved the song and put it on my album and got Leonard noticed in a way. He said to me, 'I don't understand why you're not writing your own songs.' I started writing after that."**
>
> Judy Collins

piano and sang, but she put that in the background when she married my father.

She was an excellent seamstress and a wonderful cook. She made this heavenly divinity and fudge, and those were always in the house.

My mother was a great reader. She was a member of this book club called the Opsimath Club. The word itself means something like "continuing to learn late into life." It was a selective club; the members decided that when they died, they would be cremated. As each member died, her ashes would be added to the others' ashes — no spouses' ashes were allowed in the urn. We never knew what happened to the urn.

She was a docent in a museum. She was also a member of PEO, which to us was a mystery organization, since we never knew what the letters stood for. I think it might be a Methodist organization.

HC: Yes; my wife is a member.

JC: What do the letters stand for?

HC: Philanthropical Education Organization. They have a college in Iowa they support — Coe College — but they also give scholarships to students to attend colleges other than Coe.

JC: Yes. I received a scholarship from the PEO to attend McMurray College, but they were always a mystery organization to us. [Laughs.]

HC: You started out playing classical piano. What lured you to folk music?

JC: When I was growing up, I had access to all the music in the world because of my father's collection and his radio show. I heard everything from Mozart to Cole Porter and Irving Berlin, and all kinds of music from around the world.

When I was nine, my father arranged for me to take piano lessons from Dr. Antonia Brico, who had been sort of waylaid in Denver. Although I didn't know it at the time, she was already world-famous. She had had her own orchestra at Carnegie Hall. She came to Denver because it had been suggested by city officials that she be the new conductor of the Denver Symphony. When she arrived, they told her she could not conduct the orchestra because she was a woman, which strikes me as absurd, of course, because wouldn't you think they'd have known all along that she was a woman?

She went on to form the Denver Businessman's Orchestra. I studied Mozart with her, and I played a concerto with her orchestra.

When I was about 15, I heard "The Gypsy Rover" and "Barbara Allen" on the radio. Of course, I had already been listening to the great English ballads. I asked my father to find me a guitar, since a guitar was an essential part of the folksinger's outfit [laughs], and I learned those two songs.

I was still taking piano lessons and playing Rachmaninoff, Liszt, and Mozart, but my heart belonged to the songs by Pete Seeger, the Clancy Brothers, and Woody Guthrie that I was leaning to play on the guitar. I stopped taking piano lessons, started playing in clubs in Colorado, and eventually moved to the place where I had to be if I was going to be a folksinger — New York City. By the time I was 21, I had a deal with a record label [Elektra] and put out my first album, *A Maid of Constant Sorrow.*

HC: Did you start writing songs then, too?

JC: No; I did absolutely no songwriting. At the time, no one encouraged me to write songs, nor did it seem necessary to do it. I mean, there were already all these great songs being written by Dylan, Ricky Farina, Woody, Pete, and Tom Paxton. I was a singer, and songs found their way to me. People knew they could come to me with their songs.

My father gave me the ability to recognize good songs. If you could get a song on one of my albums, you knew your song would be heard by a large audience.

Phil Ochs said to me one time, "I have to bring this guy to you; you need to hear him." He brought over Eric Andersen, and Eric went into my bathroom and finished the song he was writing, which turned out to be "Thirsty Boots." In 1973, Nancy Bacall, a close friend I met through Leonard Cohen, called me one day and told me she had found a song I had to sing by this guy named Stephen Sondheim. That's how I got "Send in the Clowns." I fell in love with his music and of course recorded an entire album of his songs.

No, I didn't start writing songs until I was about 27. Leonard Cohen came to my house, and he sang me "Suzanne." I loved the song and put it on my album and got Leonard noticed in a way. He said to me, "I don't understand why you're not writing your own songs." I started writing after that. The first song that I wrote was "Since You've Asked," and then other songs like "Albatross" and "My Father."

HC: Leonard Cohen had a huge impact on you. What were his most memorable traits?

JC: He was the real deal. His songs, like "Bird on a Wire," "Story of Isaac," and "Suzanne," are all part of my life. He and I just hit it off right away. He was a person you could really trust.

HC: You're touring with Stephen Stills and releasing a new album with him. How did that come about?

JC: It's been a dream come true. We met in 1968 in California. I had already started to write and had come out with *Wildflowers*. My record company wanted me to go back to the boards, and my producer said to Stephen, "Why don't you go play on Judy's album?" We had an affair, of course, and he sweetly wrote that little song for me, "Suite: Judy Blue Eyes."

Over the course of the years we've stayed friends, and we've been talking about doing this all those years. Finally, each of us had a window in our schedule, so we started listing songs that we wanted on the album. Stephen told me he wanted to sing my "River of Gold," and I couldn't be more thrilled that Stephen Stills wants to sing one of my songs. So, we got in the studio and had a great time.

Stephen is such a dear friend. When I had a broken heart, I would run down and get consolation from Mr. Stills.

HC: What women have most influenced you?

JC: I was very fortunate to be able to participate in some of the earliest music festivals. I had the chance to work with Ronnie Gilbert and Cynthia Gooding — Cynthia was a real inspiration to me.

Antonia Brico really shaped me. She was a ferocious woman who broke through every barrier. She conducted the Berlin Philharmonic Orchestra, the San Francisco Symphony, and the Hamburg Philharmonic. She was the first woman to conduct the New York Philharmonic. She was strict, but she was warm. In 1975 I helped make a movie about her, *Antonia: A Portrait of a Woman,* which was nominated for an Academy Award. My movie changed her life, and the Mostly Mozart Festival and the Brooklyn Philharmonic invited her to conduct after the movie came out.

HC: Did you face any challenges as a woman in the folk revival?

JC: You know, I felt many things. I felt misery, [I was] depressed. I hated the war. I lost custody of my son, Clark, in 1965, in spite of everybody telling me that courts never take custody away from the mother. Well, it happened to me, and I was devastated. I never felt marginalized or abused, though. In part because I'm very strong. I was a girl who was absolutely adored and respected by her father. Did that make a difference? I think so!

Listen, men are men, and they will always take advantage of you if they can. I think it's also this business we're in. Artists are always taken advantage of. I think it starts with money. Nobody wants to pay for music anymore. They want it for free, and labels take advantage of artists whenever they can. Artists certainly never get what they deserve. I speak out about things. As a woman who sees what happens to others, I just can't shut up about things.

HC: You have long been involved in social activism. In what ways are you active today?

JC: My activism has become personal. When my son committed suicide in 1992, I was devastated. I discovered how many people were affected by depression and suicide and how our culture simply neglected these issues. I began writing and speaking in these areas, and continue to do so. I told my story in my book *Sanity and Grace: A Journey of Suicide, Survival, and Strength.*

I am now an activist in the area of food and eating disorders. My new book, *Cravings,* came out earlier this year, and I tell about my own struggles with my own eating disorders. I realized that my food problems came from eating sugar, grain, corn, and flour, and when I cut those out of my diet, my life changed. I began to see the connections in the ways big businesses push these food items in their advertising and in the ways they try to convince us to include them in our diets. We have a big problem. A huge percentage of our culture is morbidly obese, and its due to our lack of control of our diets.

I'm all about solutions. I believe that one person can make a difference. We have a responsibility to the planet. If you change yourself, you can change the planet.

HC: What advice would you give to young women trying to make it in the music business today?

JC: Perhaps as a young woman its harder than ever to make it in music, for many of the reasons we've talked about already. The main thing is not to be discouraged. To be an artist is to struggle; that's what it's about. We who make music bring beauty and blessing to the planet. It saves your life.

HC: Can music still move the world?

JC: Yes, of course — it moves *my* world. It can be tremendously uplifting.

Making music is a service to other people. Music and art are here so that we can stay on the planet. Otherwise, what's the point?

Always resist; always play music. The fact that we can make beauty on this fundament keeps on the lights. ∎

TIME FEEDS UPON THE LIVING

The Karen Dalton no man knew

by Justin Joffe

"No woman is a passive object. We all make really strong and painful decisions, and they get overlooked a lot. I've gotten this weird compliment before: 'You're a force of nature.' Actually, no, I'm not some primal, emotional animal. I'm a person who has made choices."

Larkin Grimm

WHEN AN ARTIST lives her life in relative obscurity, gives next to no interviews, and knows from experience the vagabond-roving stories she sings, her essence risks being defined by mystery rather than certainty, objectified by hearsay rather than illuminated by truth. Karen Dalton passed away almost 25 years ago, but it wasn't until a decade later that the story of her life and untimely death was widely shared.

Originally from Enid, Oklahoma, Dalton left her home state during the 1950s, leaving behind two children and two failed marriages, though not much is known about how, when, or why. She recorded just two studio albums during her career, neither of which featured any of her original compositions, though her covers of songs like "When a Man Loves a Woman" and "It Hurts Me Too" displayed a power of their own.

As a self-described song stylist, she collected the most heartbreaking lyrical threads and riffs from folk and blues heroes, stitching them together in new arrangements and interpretations that telegraphed her innermost feelings. An incredibly private person, her journals reveal her struggles with love, motherhood, and addiction in the form of poetry, prose, and unfinished songs. All but lost among her things, those words didn't shed light on her compositional brilliance until years after she had passed.

Dalton's voice was singular — an earthen, cornmeal-crackling croon fortified by the words of those she admired and augmented by a wispy, jazzy delivery. She's been called "Hillbillie Holiday" in reference to her voice's hornlike quality, which borrowed more from jazz vocalists like Billie Holiday and Sarah Vaughan than Judy Collins, Joni Mitchell, or other prominent folksingers of her day. More than her tall stature or striking Cherokee features, it was the forlorn Oklahoma husk in her voice that helped Dalton stand out among the myriad artists swarming Greenwich Village when she arrived there in the 1960s.

In his 2004 memoir *Chronicles*, Bob Dylan called Dalton his favorite singer, having met her when he occasionally backed her up on his harmonica at venues like Gerde's Folk City. She was married to folksinger Richard Tucker and played frequent gigs with artists like Tim Hardin, and much of the story of her life and career has been told through her relationships and collaborations with these men.

Men helped frame her legacy, too. Matt Sullivan, founder of Light in the Attic Records, reissued her two studio albums — 1969's *It's Hard to Tell Who's Going to Love You the Best* and 1971's *In My Own Time* — over a decade after her death. Mark Linn of Delmore Recordings released one of her rehearsal tapes, titled *1966*, as well as a live set from 1962 called *Cotton Eyed Joe* and her home-recorded demos from 1962-'63, titled *Green Rocky Road.*

After they reconnected in the '80s, Dalton's longtime friend and fellow musician Peter Walker helped set her up with a place to live. It was there where she died a decade after contracting the AIDS virus from intravenous drug use.

Walker also published a short biography on Dalton in 2012, accompanied by a selection of her unpublished words. *Songs, Poems, Writings* sheds light on the details of Dalton's life, as only Walker knew it. Many of his remembrances are filtered through his admitted subjectivity, long lapses in not knowing where she was or what she was doing, and the fact that he knew nothing of her drug use.

A Song Collector

Peter Walker met Dalton in 1961, when she appeared with her then-husband Richard Tucker to storm what Walker perceived to be an otherwise amateur Boston folk scene. He wouldn't realize until many years later that she had been collecting the material she performed since childhood. (He found her well-worn, dog-eared copy of Alan Lomax's *Folk Songs of North America* compendium after she passed.) He says that Dalton was one of the most authentic sources of material for the folk boom, and her collection is as important as Lomax's to the survival of

those music traditions.

"It was the beginning of the '60s and people were looking around for a genuine American heritage in a fast-emerging postwar, plastic world," he writes. "Television was dumbing down America, and authentic root folk sources like Karen Dalton were the last remnants of a different era. The last of the old-time singers from a world of oral tradition which predated both radio and television was giving way to a new generation of musicians."

Dalton's knack for picking out particularly devastating lyrics provided her an outlet for her to share her own story, too. Her arrangement of the traditional "Katie Cruel," for example, tells a story of a woman who used to be a "roving jewel" until the those who knew her "changed their tune" and came to call her Katie Cruel. Considering that friends often called Dalton "KD" for short, her rendition plays as a stunningly self-aware, deliberate commentary on her own transience: "If

I was where I would be, then I'd be where I am not," she croons over her arrestingly gorgeous and mournful banjo. "Here I am where I must be. Where I would be, I cannot."

In her journal, Dalton shared details:

"Take advantage of the opportunity to spend time away in the country, away from distractions caused by diverse needs," she wrote. "Use the time to create a new mythology, to recreate a panorama of vision, enlarging, specifying, painting, pointing out a larger vision then [sic] what you lost."

After they met, Walker didn't see Dalton for a couple of years until she returned to Cambridge in 1963, having spent most of her time gigging around the country with the folksinger and songwriter Tim Hardin. He remembers her coming by the Cambridge Folk Center in Harvard Square, sitting in on jams and contributing a riff on guitar or a lick on banjo now and again. Before long, Walker left Boston too, traveling around a while before landing in New York, where he reunited with Dalton at Hardin's place in 1967.

The roving ways of these itinerant folksingers weren't particularly unusual in the '60s, when a whole generation often left their homes and families behind to travel the land in pursuit of a deeper consciousness. Even so, Walker's account does little to explain why Dalton left her home in Oklahoma as a young 20-something determined to make it as a folksinger in New York.

Dalton's daughter, Abbe Baird, once shared a story her mother told her after they reconnected years later. "She was living with a guy who caught her in bed with my eventual stepfather, and she got punched in the face," Baird told a reporter in 2012. "She used to say she was going to get her teeth fixed when she got to be a big star."

A Great, Great Sorrow

In all her travels, Dalton seems to have made few close women friends. Among them was Jill Byrem, who learned a lot about Dalton after renting her a room in the late '60s. Dalton moved into Byrem's house in Los Angeles at San Vicente and Sunset with her then-partner John Mornier, whom she had met years earlier in Boston. Before moving into Byrem's house, the pair spent several months living with Cheech Marin, who had been stashing bushels of marijuana in the attic with his friend Tommy Chong.

"One time I walked in the bedroom where she was staying, and the ivy had come right in her room," Byrem remembers. "She'd left the window open, and the ivy was climbing right up the walls. She said, 'You know, if the vibrations are good enough the plants will come right in the house after you.'"

Though that was a bright memory, Byrem notes that the spiritual joyousness it conveys couldn't coexist with Dalton's darker side. In the year and a half that they lived together, Dalton overdosed twice. Ten days after one incident, when Byrem called Dalton an ambulance, she remembers Dalton giving her a call and saying, 'It's taken me almost two weeks to thank you.'"

Unlike Peter Walker, Byrem had become close enough to Dalton to see the extent of her addiction. She later became a well-respected country singer in her own right, changing her name to Lacy J. Dalton in honor of her close friendship with Karen. Often, Byrem recalls, Dalton confided about how torn up she was over having left behind a son and daughter in Enid.

"She did not have her children with her, and that was a great, great sorrow," Byrem says. "She loved those children and missed them terribly. It ate her alive

"It was the beginning of the '60s and people were looking around for a genuine American heritage in a fast-emerging postwar, plastic world. Television was dumbing down America, and authentic root folk sources like Karen Dalton were the last remnants of a different era."

Peter Walker

that she was not able to tell them how much she loved them and why she had to do what she had to do. I think that was a terrible, terrible burden for her."

Dalton addressed that burden in her personal journals, through a deeply analytical and spiritual lens. She alluded to the metaphysical concepts of harmony embedded in her Cherokee heritage while simultaneously extracting her own philosophies from them.

"If the main worth of creation lies not with the creator but in expanded energy, time, direction, [and] will used to create it, what basis for worth is there once it's done," she wrote. "A shirt for baby, finished after baby's outgrown the size, has worth because of intention, of thought and planning and eventual conceptual becoming concrete. Does possibility of using it for another child still small enough endow finished shirt with worth? What if there were no future baby's [sic] and shirt had no purpose except pleasing to look at and to touch. Our need for harmony gives us desire for items with no utilitarian purpose as such. But the state of mind engendered through looking at pleasing creation is (in a sense) utilitarian (especially to someone seeking the state of mind it

sways.) Thus paintings made to change consciousness."

Using the words of these unpublished writings as a starting point, Josh Rosenthal's Tompkins Square Records released a compilation in 2015 that set Dalton's poems and unfinished songs to music. *Remembering Mountains: The Unheard Songs of Karen Dalton* features only women — Lucinda Williams, Sharon Van Etten, and Patty Griffin among them — who give Dalton's unsung words life through new arrangements and melodies.

Singer-songwriter Larkin Grimm performed "For the Love I'm In" on *Remembering Mountains,* and says she particularly connected with the lyrics as a mother. "It's this song about stealing a beautiful moment in the midst of a painful life," Grimm says. "Something as simple as taking a long walk is this incredible relief. I feel like that song is about having a love affair, but it also speaks deeply to womanhood. When I first became a mom, these moments of being able to step outside the house without my child and just take a walk, just go around the block, felt incredible. Such freedom to just walk alone. I don't even think men think about that.

"The establishment is not built for

women or women's needs," she continues. "It doesn't allow you to be a mom. It doesn't even allow you to be pregnant. And when Karen Dalton made that decision to leave her kids behind — there's no going back. Every time you're onstage you must be thinking about your kids, what they're doing, where they are. It's a strong thing to do, because you're always gonna have that pain. That bond of love never dissolves, and I imagine it gave Karen a lot of power and soul.

"People like to talk about how she had a hard life, and was an addict, that's why she was soulful," Grimm adds. "No — it's because she was a mother."

Byrem takes a different angle. "I don't think it made her strong," she says. "I think it was the great sorrow of her life. She couldn't forgive herself for it. That's one of the reasons she self-medicated.

"She would be talking about her son or her daughter, and a tear would come down her cheek. I don't think she thought she could support those children doing what she did. But she was also born to do what she did, and when you have a calling like that, sometimes those choices are made. How you live with those choices is your own hell."

stick my cowboy boot all the way up your ass. I hate this place. You're gonna get me a plane ticket back to New York City and you're gonna do it *now*. And somebody oughtta change their name.'"

That was the last time she and Karen Dalton ever spoke. Byrem never knew that her friend had passed away from AIDS until contacted for this story.

At Final Parting

Peter Walker says that one day in the early '90s, when Dalton had moved from her jailed friend's house into a trailer down the road, a social worker showed up to check on her. Always hospitable, Dalton invited her in. The social worker noticed an appliance cord running behind the kitchen sink, and made that the basis for an argument that Dalton was not of sound mind and body and, as such, ought to be placed in the care of the state. When Dalton learned about that, she called Walker. "I want to die at home," she told him.

Having earned his paralegal certificate from Baruch College years before, Walker was permitted to argue on someone's behalf in the state and county social service system. He remembers telling an all-female committee that Karen was in the private care of an excellent doctor, and requested he be on record as saying, "I can't believe that … you, a group of women, in this day and age of liberation and freedom of choice for women, would deny this person, a woman, the right to die in her own home."

Walker and Dalton reunited in Woodstock, New York, in 1970. On Walker's frequent trips upstate, he brought his children to visit Dalton, who was then staying in a spare room with mutual friend Bob Brainen. She loved his children as though they were her own, and spent a good deal of time with them until her AIDS-related illnesses began to surface in the early '80s.

During that decade, Dalton's story became convoluted. Walker maintains that she had an apartment in the Bronx, which she afforded by taking odd jobs like passing out fliers, plus a house upstate, near Hudson, which was vacated by a friend of hers after he went to jail.

In the late '80s, Byrem heard that Dalton was out on the street, that her teeth had fallen out due to her addiction. Byrem called her friend Tom Metcalf, who ran a drug treatment facility in Denton, Texas. He agreed to treat Dalton, so Byrem fetched Dalton's cat from Pennsylvania, got her guitars out of hock, and bought her a ticket to Dallas. Byrem and Metcalf had paid for a recording session, for when Dalton's treatment was completed, and planned to fix her teeth.

Byrem remembers that Dalton stayed in treatment for just two days before bailing on the whole thing. Over the phone she told Byrem, "I oughtta

Walker's argument eventually persuaded the state of New York, and he agreed to allow a social worker to come over weekly to check on Dalton. A little over a week later he got a note that the social worker wanted to come by for a visit. He hugged Dalton goodnight, and notes now that he "was surprised at how thin she was, and the wave of heat that emanated from her frail form." When Walker went to see her the next day, she had passed.

"One time she was crying because she felt many of her friends had deserted her," says Walker now. "I held her in my arms, brushed away a tear from her cheek and remember going, 'If I kiss away this tear from her cheek, will I get AIDS from the body fluid?'

"People just didn't know, and they were afraid," he adds. "She was in a lovely house with a view and a heated swimming pool. But the fear of AIDS was so great that after she died, they filled in the pool."

"Time feeds upon the living," Dalton wrote in her journal.

What else did addiction serve
Not easing pain, it's not like most
often depicted
Get hurt by a lover,
so get high to ease the pain
Maybe its so subtly hooking
because it's easy to be devoted
To thrust all that misplaced love,
that spirited charade that captured
shadow, to capture to grab all to
myself a mold-able flexible
reinforcing risk you can't risk.
Instead of spending lifetimes

learning the songs of silence.
The descent of desire, one can short
cut, short cut — one can use the
frozen food the instant potatoes the
pat passion/One can shout Death is
the universe, the universal equalizer.

Singer-songwriter Marissa Nadler, who contributed "So Long Ago and Far Away" to *Remembering Mountains*, isn't sure why Dalton never sang any of her own work, despite its brilliance.

"When you're predominantly known as a vocalist in the older tradition, you have a band and you're supplied songs," says Nadler. "Maybe she was just sticking to the tradition of her role. You're talking about an era where it wasn't that easy for women. It still isn't. Maybe somebody told her to just stick to the vocals."

"No woman is a passive object," adds Larkin Grimm. "We all make really strong and painful decisions, and they get overlooked a lot. I've gotten this weird compliment before: 'You're a force of nature.' Actually, *no,* I'm not some primal, emotional animal. I'm a person who has made choices."

One of Dalton's unpublished poems brings these choices to light with a spiritually illuminated window into her practice:

Words that go together well are
Like those fine phrases
Used with sullen gazes
At someone you used to know.
And at final parting noting
Which words you choose to say
The things you choose to say.

Those words that go together well
Are areas worth taming
And the taming sometimes changes
But always rearranges
The things you choose to lose.

These words reveal that before Dalton died, she accepted all her choices, from leaving her children behind in Enid, Oklahoma, to self-medicating with hard drugs. Dalton didn't make those choices as one man's Cherokee muse or a "force of nature" either — she made them as a singer, a song stylist, an archivist of dying oral traditions, a collector of words that moved her, a poet, and a mother.

It's impossible to separate the artist from the art, as Dalton put her whole self into every song she sang, infusing the words of others with personal moments of joy, pain, and memory. Through her vast collection of other people's songs, she nurtured her own mystery, and as her personal life began to adversely affect her career, the two became interwoven, inseparable. Songs became meditations on Dalton's own transience when she sang them, fleeting moments when the audience had no choice but to be present with her.

"She knew who she was," says Walker. "Once I asked her, 'Karen, you think you're gonna be one of those people who's gonna be famous after you die?' 'Well, it won't make any difference to me,' she said, 'I won't be around to enjoy it.'" ∎

Additional reporting was provided by Gwendolyn Elliott.

READY FOR JOY

As America grapples with dark days, Ruthie Foster offers comfort

by Mike Seely

IN A MUSIC VIDEO FILMED IN A small white chapel on Willie Nelson's Luck Ranch in the Texas Hill Country, a diminutive middle-aged black woman with a full head of dreadlocks peers out at the sunshine from a window.

"I want to be ready," she sings, "when joy comes back to me."

When she's finished singing, she walks outside the church, her hands full of large placards with words written on them in marker. There, she's joined by her young daughter before the camera shifts to various Austin locales, where local scenesters are shown holding placards of their own, each meant to signify the things they find most comforting and healing in this world.

Gospel music. Tacos. Tater tots. Pajamas. Free time, Understanding. Singing harmony. Pizza. Books. Babies. Playing drums. Guitars. Sharing a smile. Enjoying nature with your kids. Travel. The smell of cats. Coffee. Allen Toussaint playing piano. Psilocybin. Hay. Carrots. Making stuff. Breaking stuff. These are the things that bring joy to Ruthie Foster, her daughter Maya, and their friends — which includes a pair of horses, hence the carrots and hay.

"Joy Comes Back" is the titular track

off the three-time Grammy nominee's latest album, and features a sweet guitar solo from Derek Trucks. For Trucks' wife and bandmate, Susan Tedeschi, the song conveys "such a positive message in such a negative time." It's not neuroscience to figure out what she's referring to: A billionaire blowhard with tangerine skin and the diplomatic skills of a preschooler has taken much of America's joy. How, then, does one get it back?

Enveloping oneself in Foster's stunningly versatile oeuvre is a fine place to start. Foster adroitly plays blues, gospel, country, folk, jazz, and even rock, her precise diction and vocal elasticity virtually unrivaled among her peers.

"She might have the most powerful voice in Austin," says Warren Hood, who plays mandolin and fiddle on *Joy Comes Back*.

But it's Janiva Magness, one of the few musicians to rival Foster's stylistic dexterity, who cuts to the core of Foster's appeal. "There is a kind comfort coming from her music that puts the listener at ease almost immediately," says Magness. "She makes me smile on the inside."

Comfort. It's a little different than joy, but a necessary precursor nonetheless. And when the chips are down, Foster's music is the sort that can make you see the light again, a pillowy bosom to bury your tear-streaked face in, a flannel shirt that soaks up the moisture as you refocus on the hard road ahead.

And to think a nascent career ordering parts for naval helicopters nearly robbed the world of such a resource.

Gospel and Sabbath

If a fire were to start at Santa Monica's legendary McCabe's Guitar Shop, it would stand to reason that staffers would rush to evacuate the store's extremely expensive collection of stringed instruments. But that's not what Lincoln Myerson would make off with. Instead, he'd stuff his arms — or, better yet, an enormous duffel bag — with the framed photos in the upstairs hallway.

The mustachioed Myerson, who resembles D-Day from *Animal House,* is the booker at McCabe's. And, oh, the roster of artists he and his predecessors have booked over the past half-century. Lucinda Williams, Tom Petty, Chrissie Hynde, Bonnie Raitt, Beck, Joni Mitchell, Tom Waits, J.J. Cale, Kasey Chambers, John Hiatt, Vince Gill, Jackson Browne, Linda Ronstadt, Cowboy Junkies — they're all in action before a room of fans on folding chairs, captured in black and white in the portraits.

In an uncluttered room off the shop's hallway, Foster is seated comfortably on an old sofa that nearly swallows her slight frame, reminiscing about how she got her start a few hours before she's to play a sold-out show on a Saturday night.

Foster grew up in a huge family in the tiny Texas town of Gause, a short drive from College Station. Her "paw paw," as she calls her grandfather, loved *Hee Haw* and a cappella music, and her home was filled with the sounds of gospel.

"I lived in a black part of town; it was pretty clear that's what it was," she says. "I didn't grow up with racism any more than anyone else did, but even in that small town, there were seven churches, and there was a lot of segregation going on. But I guess you could say I helped integrate the churches by being the first African-American singer to play in those churches."

Foster attended community college in Waco, where she sang in a blues band. But she yearned to see what life was like outside the Lone Star State, and "wanted a break from music." When she visited a local military recruiters' office, she recalls that the Marine rep looked too serious, but that the naval officer had his feet up on the desk.

"He was just chillin'," says Foster. So she joined the Navy.

Foster was stationed in San Diego, where her job was to order parts for helicopters. There was "something about keeping things in order" that appealed to Foster. But, alas, she concedes, "Music was callin' me."

She decided to join a pickup band on the base, and soon found herself singing Jimi Hendrix's "Red House" at a party for an executive officer. The XO was blown away, and called Foster into his office a few days later. He asked her why she was in the Navy. She told him she was there to order helicopter parts. He said, "No, you're not," and shipped her off to the Naval School of Music in Virginia, where she performed with an official military band.

Upon completing her service, Foster decamped for New York City, where she played various folk venues and was soon signed to Big Beat, an urban-leaning imprint of Atlantic Records.

"They were looking for a mix between a Tracy Chapman and Anita Baker," Foster recalls. "Record labels tend to herd you toward a genre with suggestions of people to write with. The material I turned in, they weren't interested in. And I turned in a lot of songs."

In three years with the label, Foster never recorded a single tune, and subsequently moved back to Texas to care for her ailing mother. After her mom died in 1996, Foster became a central figure in

Austin's exploding roots music scene, playing such venues as Threadgill's, the Saxon Pub, Stubb's, Maria's Tacos, and Antone's, where she would eventually cut a well-received live album on Blue Corn Music, which has been her label since 2002.

"If you lived in Austin and listened to KGSR — which is nothing like the KGSR of today — you'd hear Ruthie Foster, then Robert Earl Keen, then the Jayhawks, Lyle Lovett, Lucinda Williams," says Dan Barrett, who plays in the local band Porterdavis and produced *Joy Comes Back*. "Ruthie and Bob Schneider and a couple other folks just captured the zeitgeist of this town at a really golden age of roots music in Austin. Eight years later, we found ourselves living in the same neighborhood."

Foster loves playing live. That affinity does not extend to the studio, however.

"You're basically locked in a room with a glass window and all you see is the top of the producer's head while they're looking at this board," Foster explains. "It's not as inspiring to sing and create for me as a vocalist. It is like a job in that way. Being a professional, I know how to turn it on and give the best performance I can, but it'll never be what it's gonna be live when it comes to the emotion behind it."

After an extensive European tour, Foster says, "The last thing I wanted to do was get back in the studio. But I knew Dan, and he made this great coffee on the French press." Barrett also had a studio, and Foster — an in-demand guest singer — needed a place to lay some vocals down.

After a year of hanging out, Foster decided to cut the Deb Talan track "Forgiven" with Barrett at the controls.

" 'Forgiven' opened up a new way to sing for me," says Foster. "It was more of a songwriter's song that I connected to. I'd done songwriter's songs that I loved melodically. This song I connected with lyrically first, and I hadn't done that with a cover in a long time."

There was a profound reason for this synergy: Foster had just broken off a long-term relationship with the co-parent of her 6-year-old daughter. She'd lost her joy, and needed a way to get it back. The first step was forgiveness, and what followed was a typically rangy album that includes imaginative covers of Stevie Wonder, Chris Stapleton, and, improbably, Black Sabbath's "War Pigs."

Foster's interest in metal is no passing fancy, and she's got her old naval colleagues to thank for that. "They were schooling me on Deep Purple," she explains, "and that's how I got into Black Sabbath."

Got It Covered

For as much respect as she commands in Austin and on the blues-award circuit, Foster is not a household name outside her loyal cadre of fans. But occasionally she creeps into more mainstream quarters, like when she joined the Allman Brothers for their legendary Beacon Theatre residency in New York — trading verses with Susan Tedeschi on a cover of "The Weight" by The Band — or when she duetted with Bonnie Raitt on "Angel from Montgomery" at a festival in Austin.

"There was so much weed," she says of her stint with the Allmans. "I was so high from second-hand smoke. I was just devouring potato chips."

As for her live collaboration with Raitt, she performed that John Prine tune before thousands of fans without the benefit of a rehearsal. Raitt recalls Foster saying, "I got it covered," adding, "When she said that, I believed her."

Raitt had been a fan of Foster's work for years before the duo finally shared a stage. "I heard about her from Taj Mahal," says Raitt of Foster's onetime tourmate. "The buzz across the blues and roots community was pretty strong, and she lived up to every accolade. One of the best shows I've ever seen was when Ruthie played Yoshi's [in Oakland, California] the night before Obama got elected."

As for Foster's following, Raitt observes, "I hope she crosses over big time, but as someone who has something of a cult following, you can last longer if you stay in the loyal fan community than with this year's model. Everybody that likes me would probably love her. Adele was nice enough to mention me [in London during a live taping, before she covered "I Can't Make You Love Me"], so it's kind of like a food chain — all of us giving props to the artists we love."

Incidentally, Foster covered Adele's "Set Fire to the Rain" on her 2011 album *Let It Burn*, and she frankly one-ups the originators on her renditions of Patty Griffin's "When It Don't Come Easy" and Lucinda Williams' "Fruits of My Labor," both of which she played before an extremely appreciative audience at McCabe's. While Williams' signature vocal attribute is a lazy Louisiana drawl, Foster slows the track down, enunciating every consonant as she gets in Williams' Mercury and drives out west, pedal to the metal and her luck to the test.

"Music is a healer for me," Foster tells those assembled in Santa Monica, and she may as well be speaking for us all. ∎

LOST AND FOUND

Artists who have re-emerged strike a chord with Sharon Van Etten

by Cameron Matthews

SINGER-SONGWRITER Sharon Van Etten emerged in the early aughts with frightening composure, vivid lyrics on the horrors of having to feel and give love, and a low alto that could perform high-flying vocal gymnastics without warning. The New Jersey native has no epic origin story or fable when it comes to happening upon the folk and country music that's intimately woven into her compositions. In fact, she discovered it the same way so many others of her generation have — sitting in a car with a friend and a mix CD, in some half-deserted parking lot, in some rural county, smoking cigarettes with the windows rolled halfway down.

Van Etten took several detours before betting it all on Brooklyn, where she eventually became a songwriting staple in the local indie scene. In 1999, she ventured far from her home in New Jersey to study recording at Middle Tennessee State University in Murfreesboro. It was here, in the South, that the soft-spoken singer found the essence of her sound, along with a record's full of heartbreak, which she would release under the title *epic*.

Van Etten quit school after a year, opting instead for a real-world education at the Red Rose, a coffee shop that doubled as a venue and proving ground for a lot of young artists. It was around this time that she fell into the deep end of a truly abusive relationship — a subject she's written quite a bit about. "This guy didn't even let me have a guitar," she told *Spin's* David Marchese back in 2011.

Van Etten escaped back to her parents' basement in New Jersey, where a seven-track, breakout sophomore album poured out of her. *epic* (Ba Da Bing Records, 2010) explores the hell of bad matches and painful transitions, all with the sparseness of an acoustic guitar and Van Etten's otherworldly crooning, earning her comparisons to the soaring vocals of Roy Orbison and the spurting-vein lyricism of Bon Iver.

After *Tramp* (Jagjaguwar, 2012) and *Are We There* (Jagjaguwar, 2014), it's difficult to compare Van Etten thematically to anyone else when it comes to matters of the heart. Her four full-length albums explore the chasms of limerence and lonesomeness with such painstaking detail and melodic charm that even Bill Monroe, known for his high lonesome vocals, might have marveled at her ability to channel such relatable feelings into music.

In recent years, disillusioned by a never-ending tour schedule, Van Etten has taken several unexpected detours, first by going back to school to become a mental health counselor — a fitting occupation given her emotional experience. She has since withdrawn from school (for now) to pursue a blossoming acting career. She played an abductee named Rachel on the cult Netflix hit, *The OA,* in which she inherits a powerful singing voice after surviving a near-death experience. Van Etten also cameos on the latest revival season of *Twin Peaks*, earning her more than a bit of weirdo cred.

But there aren't many detours quite like her latest creative endeavor: becoming a mom. Van Etten spoke to me by phone from her home in Brooklyn, where I could hear her 10-week-old baby, Denver, cooing patiently in his mom's arms. With many years of heartache behind her, she's excited to write new music, motivated not by the pain of a bad relationship, but by the prospects of parenthood.

Though it wouldn't be exactly true to call the now-36-year-old a roots musician, her music is still highly influenced by artists who are outsiders and weirdos — a tradition in American

music often overlooked when journalists are digging into what constitutes folk and country music.

For Van Etten, there are four distinct oddballs that have moved her more than the Dollies and Lorettas of the world. These outsiders are obscure, sure, and some of them have been widely forgotten, but Van Etten is not alone in her praise for their work, nor in the way she's channeled their influence into her own art. For artists of her generation, who are more compelled by music they love than they are by any specific category, it makes sense to take a moment and nod toward the women who have carried on the outsider artist tradition in American music.

The first among those whom Van Etten cites as her foremothers, English singer-songwriter Vashti Bunyan, godmother of freak folk, was almost entirely forgotten

after disappointing sales of her first album in 1970 led her to abandon music until her rediscovery in the early 2000s. Sibylle Baier, the German equivalent of Molly Drake, made stunning home recordings for nothing more than her own amusement. Elyse Weinberg enjoyed fame in and around Laurel Canyon, recording with Neil Young, JD Souther, and Nils Lofgren until she unceremoniously walked away from it all. And Kentucky-born recording artist Jackie DeShannon performed several major hits like "What the World Needs Now Is Love," and "Put a Little Love in Your Heart," yet remains a hidden gem in our modern times.

Van Etten was unabashed about her connection to these songwriters and singers that have their own specific

kinship, woven into our culture's forgetfulness and obsession with rediscovery. Our interview has been edited for continuity.

CAMERON MATTHEWS: Vashti Bunyan, in 1970, only sold a few copies of her record, *Just Another Diamond Day,* and then she abandoned music for 30 years while riding this kind of cult following. Then she re-emerged around 2000 or so and began putting out music again. As somebody who has gone through some significant life transitions recently, do you feel a kind of kinship with her?

SHARON VAN ETTEN: When I first heard her, I was probably in my early 20s. My friend put her on a mix CD for me. I didn't know anything about her backstory until I moved back up North. That's when I lived in Tennessee. But now, of course, more and more, I am connecting to her music because it was almost like she had this secret life. I wonder what my son will think of what I do and if, by the time he grows up, I will still be doing what I'm doing when he is old enough to understand. I still don't know.

CM: It's interesting that you came to her later in life, because the vocal similarities alone between the two of you are ghostly. I assume that you had already sort of solidified the sound of your voice, which presents itself as a very clear whisper, yet steady like a woodwind. When you first heard her, did you think, "That sounds like me"?

SVE: It was funny. My friend Rebecca, who's done artworks for my first two records, she has turned me on to a lot of music over the years. Before I was really performing out and I was just in my bedroom playing songs for friends that wouldn't encourage me, she put Vashti Bunyan and Sibylle Baier on the same mix CD for me. Typically, [it's] what I listened to until I moved back east to Jersey to get my life back in order while living with my parents. I definitely connected with their voices.

As I have more distance between us, I'm realizing the similarities in our voices, how they're quiet, how they're lower, how they're wispy, how they're melodic. Again, they kept it pretty private

and didn't have aspirations to be something bigger than they are. Beyond the music, with hindsight, I connect very deeply with their path.

CM: You told *Spin* a couple years ago: "I love everyone I work with, but how am I going to have the time to step away and have a life to even write about?" It feels like these women that put out these records decades ago really were filled with life. I assume that there's a point where you keep going back to the well and maybe there's nothing there until you find your own way again, right?

SVE: Right. In general, if you're a creative spirit, the muse comes and goes. Sometimes it's from traveling too much, from being tired. It's from needing space or not having a routine. It can stem from many things.

Sometimes it takes me time to start writing and singing and having something to write about. Sometimes it was there all along. I think it's where you're at emotionally and mentally.

CM: I want to ask you about place and how it can influence songwriting. You grew up in New Jersey and became a songwriter in Tennessee, and then you moved to Brooklyn. What sort of songwriters were you listening to in college in the South? I can only assume that you were getting a little bit of twang influence.

SVE: Well it's kind of funny, actually.

My Tennessee influence was mostly punk rock, hardcore, emo, math rock. But it wasn't until later that I got a little bit of an education on Loretta Lynn and Dolly Parton. It was a time when more indie rock and alternative rock [were] passing through, more so than country, where I was. And in some ways I'm very glad because I don't know if I was ready for it at the time. I had a lot of angst that I needed to get out. I'm glad that I came to it when I was writing more actively. It wasn't until the end of my time in Tennessee [that] my friend Rebecca turned me on to Vashti Bunyan [and others]. I didn't listen to much folk music back then. I know that's unexpected.

CM: Sibylle Baier has a very interesting discovery story.

SVE: I believe it was her son that found the tapes that her friends made her record. Again, this is just from what I'm pulling from my memory from years ago.

CM: Yeah! Her son Robby, ... I guess she made a couple of tapes for people, and he digitized them. Then he actually passed it on to J Mascis of Dinosaur Jr., who then gave it to Orange Twin Records.

SVE: Really? I didn't know that.

CM: And Baier's most popular song, "Tonight," is a real trip. It sounds like a slacker wrote it, but as you get deeper, it gets sadder, and, weirdly, even more mundane. The lyrics themselves, like:

> **"It may take some time, but I'm realizing that I don't need that broken heart to be my muse all the time. "**
>
> Sharon Van Etten

Tonight, when I came home from work
there he, unforeseen
sat in the kitchen
buttering himself a bread
The cat was on his knee
and smiled at me.

It reminds me of how you write, using a journalistic approach. When did you first start toying around with that method?

SVE: I didn't grow up being a very good storyteller. I go back to the class assignments where I'm supposed to write a piece of fiction, and I laugh at stories I tried to make up. They weren't very believable, if I can be honest. Whenever I try to tell a story that isn't mine, I think they sound terrible. It's hard to connect to them. I've always struggled with that.

When I was learning how to write songs, I just wanted it to be like I was talking to somebody, because I didn't want it to be overly poetic. I don't think that comes naturally to me. I think it's more of trying to put things in simple terms about what I'm feeling and then trying to find a language that keeps it from being too specific, where someone won't relate to it.

I'm like, "Oh, if someone that knew me listened to this song and knew exactly why I wrote this, then it's probably not something I should share." That was one of my rules.

Another [rule is] if I just read the lyrics on paper, does it sound like something I would say? Does it use the vocabulary I would normally use and then reach beyond that? That helped me get started, usually. If I could just boil it down to what it was that I was feeling and what I was trying to say in layman's terms.

CM: Elyse Weinberg is similar to the other artists you've listed in that she left music entirely. Her record *Greasepaint Smile* did very well, she was friends with Neil Young, had quite a few accolades. It seems that more people are influenced by her now than in the Laurel Canyon days.

SVE: I came across her music in two different ways. Someone I used to date had her album. He used to play me records and he would say, "This is a very distinct voice for this time." I would basically listen to whatever he suggested because he had really good taste in music.

She's such a strong voice, she's bluesy. I thought, "How do people not know about her?" You can Google all you want, but there's not very much information on her out there.

CM: The outlier on your list is Jackie DeShannon. Can you talk about the first time you heard her and what you think of her?

SVE: One of the first times I heard Jackie DeShannon was at a small bar in the Lower East Side. I had a crush on this guy and every time I walked in to where he was DJing, "Needles & Pins" would come on without fail. I felt like I was in a movie. It was such a sound-track-of-my-life moment for me. Her voice was so strong but she is so weak, she just lets go. The low and raspy range of her voice got me right away.

CM: Do you feel like you need to be in a specific emotional state in order to create music? Do you think you can make music from a place where you're unequivocally happy?

SVE: For a while I thought that I would only be able to write songs if I was in a tumultuous relationship, but that's not where I am now and I've been writing a lot. It's just having the courage to face exactly where you are in life. Sometimes it's hard to write about. I've always been the kind of writer that writes from personal experience and close to a journalistic style. I am learning how to look beyond that.

When you're looking at mortality and fate every day, and the embodiment is your lover, and you're looking at the product that you've made and forcing yourself to think about mortality and their future and everything, it's heavier. It's way heavier than an unhealthy relationship. It may take some time, but I'm realizing that I don't need that broken heart to be my muse all the time. ∎

Kris Delmhorst

Lori McKenna

Catie Curtis

Paula Cole

Leading Ladies

by Mark Erelli

IKE SO MANY SONGWRITERS of my generation, I owe a huge debt to the likes of Willie Nelson, Bob Dylan, and Jackson Browne. But, while I've learned a great deal from listening to their music, I've learned even more by writing with and playing alongside other artists. And for reasons I've never quite been able to discern, I've done most of my co-writing and sideman work with women.

I started out purely as a writer and singer of my own songs, but my friend (and then Signature Sounds labelmate) Kris Delmhorst hired me as a sideman. Onstage with Kris, I soon realized the biggest perk of being an accompanist is that you get the best seat in the house. Standing just a few feet away, I could more closely observe the artist at work than I ever could have in the audience.

Kris has a delicate, relaxed approach to a melody — singing with a smile on her face, she rarely raises her voice to drive home the emotional core of a song. Growing up, I consumed a steady diet of 1980s Bruce Springsteen and hair metal bombast, but Kris' gentle way with a song inspired a fundamental shift in my own music. I started seeking ways to maintain intensity in the composition and execution of a melody while dialing back the amount of energy I expend for its delivery. A couple decades later, I'm still trying to learn what Kris has seemed to always know about singing: It's always easier than I think it needs to be.

I worked with Catie Curtis next. She had already won me over as a fan several years earlier. Our relationship initially felt like being taken under the wing of a more established artist, but grew increasingly collaborative. In time, I toured the country with Catie as a sideman and opening act, but it all started by simply getting together to share our latest songs. That a widely known artist like Catie might feel she had something to learn from interacting with a less experienced writer like myself was its own revelation. But as we played for each other nascent works in varying stages of completion, the suggestion of an occasional line or chord change blossomed into full-blown co-writing. These songs appeared on one ("Here & Now") or both of our albums ("Passing Through"), and one inspired by the aftermath of Hurricane Katrina, "People Look Around," bested 15,000 entries to win the grand prize in the International Songwriting Competition. Catie taught me the value of collaboration: A shared vision can sometimes take you places you can't envision on your own.

More recently, I've had the good fortune to work with Paula Cole, whose piano-based songs like "I Don't Wanna Wait" are not only harmonically complex, but were also enormous hits on '90s pop radio. Paula is a learned, technically proficient musician, and getting under the hood of her songs required me to think outside of the typical patterns followed by folk and roots music. I had to find new tunings and different chord inversions than I'd used before, some of which inevitably found their way into my own songs.

When it came time to record my most recent album, *For A Song,* Paula graciously offered to sing on a couple of tracks. Her layered harmonies on "French King" and "Look Up" eschew the traditional approach of following a third or fifth above the melody, instead combining several interwoven harmony parts into one glorious whole that feels more akin to a string quartet. Paula taught me that when I look more closely at the harmonic possibilities presented in my songs, there is often a choice between the easy way and the deeper way, and it's always best to go deeper.

My longest-running and perhaps most educational musical friendship is with Lori McKenna, who I first met in 1996 after we both lost the same songwriting contest. I shared writers' rounds and songwriter bills with Lori before beginning to work in her band in 2004, and I now serve as its unofficial musical director. Just when I think she's said everything there is to say about her hometown, she comes up with another jewel of a song that finds a new way to witness and dignify our everyday joys and trials. Lori has showed me that the people and places closest to us, although easiest to overlook or take for granted, often provide the deepest wells of inspiration. The way she has approached her career — consistently turning down professional opportunities that would conflict with family obligations — has proved a valuable example as well. People expect male artists to hit the road constantly, luxuriating in the role of a grizzled troubadour. But Lori's approach has inspired me to recognize the importance of marriage and parenthood, and to conduct my business accordingly.

Choosing to be home a bit more often than your average road dog means a richer life with my wife and kids, which in turn often leads to better songs. The consistency of spirit and intention I've witnessed in Lori, whether we're playing for 100 people at Club Passim or thousands at the Grand Ole Opry, is one of my biggest inspirations. My work with Lori has given me the courage to follow my own road and make decisions accordingly. Music is great, she's taught me, but family is everything. ∎

EVERY HOMETOWN GIRL

Growing through life with Mary Chapin Carpenter

by Cynthia Sanz

This is an excerpt from Woman Walk the Line: How the Women in Country Music Changed Our Lives, *a collection of personal essays edited by Holly Gleason and published as part of University of Texas Press' American Music Series in September 2017.*

NEW JERSEY-BRED. IVY League-educated. More flannel shirt than frilly dress. Mary Chapin Carpenter was nothing like the female country artists I'd grown up with. And everything like the woman I was growing up to be. It was December 1990, and I was driving home to San Antonio after my first year working in New York City. Carpenter's "You Win Again" was just breaking into radio airplay. It was the first single from her 1990 album *Shooting Straight in the Dark*. And it was all of my 20-something romantic angst set to music.

> *I'm standing here freezing at a phone booth baby*
> *In the middle of God knows where.*
> *I got one quarter left, your machine picks up*
> *But baby I know you're there.*

Just one year earlier, I'd moved halfway across the country to begin work as a staff writer at *People* magazine. Living in New York City was fast-paced and exciting. I was going to fabulous parties, interviewing celebrities, and building a life for myself. But I was also single, and struggling with the dating world. A string of romances had fizzled soon after they began. Driving home that December, I heard my own life in Carpenter's aching alto.

Once called the patron saint of the single woman, Carpenter brought sensitivity and emotional depth — and a decidedly feminist perspective — to country music in the 1990s. Holding her own amidst that decade's herd of "hat acts," she sang about love and longing with a poet's voice and heart-on-her-sleeve honesty.

> *I can't be right if I'm always wrong*
> *I can't stand up if I'm always kneeling*
> *At your altar or at your throne,*
> *You could show just a little feeling*
> *For who I am*
> *Baby you win again.*

But the heroines of Carpenter's songs didn't take their heartbreak lying down. They demanded answers and walked away with their pride, if not their hearts, intact. For a generation of women like me, trying to navigate the changing currents of love and career, Carpenter was a sister-in-arms. "She gave her heart away one time, and says that she hasn't seen it since," she sang on "Middle Ground," another cut off *Shooting Straight in the Dark*. "All her single friends are men / She thinks married girls are so damn boring."

Part of Nashville's acclaimed "Class of '89," Carpenter hit the charts with a wave of new traditionalists like Garth Brooks, Clint Black, and Alan Jackson. Country was booming, and its boundaries were being pushed ever outward.

My childhood had been steeped in country music. I'd sung along to Dolly Parton, Crystal Gayle, and Reba McEntire on the radio. My family watched *Hee Haw* and *The Porter Wagoner Show* every Sunday. And my high school friends and I had two-stepped through our proms.

But Carpenter was a different kind of country artist. Melodically, her sound was closer to '70s rock and folk music, and her lyrics strayed far from country's blue-collar touchstones. She looked different, too. In a sea of sequins and hairspray, she took the stage in jeans and flannel shirts, like she'd just wandered off one of the Seven Sisters campuses. And she sang about independent women charting their own courses.

Of course, Carpenter was always an unlikely country star. The daughter of a

Life magazine exec, she had gone to prep school, lived in Tokyo while her father was working abroad, and graduated from Brown University with a degree in American civilization. Then she got her start on the coffeehouse circuit around Washington, DC.

Her first album, 1987's folky *Hometown Girl*, won critical acclaim but got little airplay. It wasn't until 1989's *State of the Heart* that Carpenter began to make her mark on country radio, with hits like the flirty "How Do?", the aching "Never Had It So Good," and the quietly regretful "Quittin' Time."

Even in those early years, Carpenter displayed an independent streak. At the 1990 Country Music Association awards, the then-32-year-old singer was invited to perform on the broadcast. But instead of singing one of her hits, she opted for a cleverly cutting song she'd been playing at her live shows: "You Don't Know Me (I'm the Opening Act)." With biting wit, the song called out a superstar "hat act" who had made opening for him on tour such an unpleasant experience that she felt compelled to write about it.

I don't have a hit on the Billboard
  charts
I don't have a limousine that
  stretches three blocks
Ready to take me from door to door
Just like that jackass I'm opening for.
He doesn't know me ...
I'm his opening act.

It was a daring move for someone so

new to the business — even without naming the song's egotistical star. But the audience's initial gasps quickly turned to cheers. The performance stole the show that night, winning the Nashville newcomer a standing ovation from the industry crowd. "It was a special opportunity and I did it," she would later recall. "I'll always remember that night. Michael Campbell, Ricky Van Shelton's manager at the time, was there during soundcheck and he was the last person I saw before I went onstage. Right before I went out, I heard him say 'That was a nice career you had going there, Carpenter!' When the audience stood and applauded, I was just flabbergasted."

Far from killing her career, the moment ignited it. Her third studio album, *Shooting Straight in the Dark,* became a critical and commercial success, launching four Top 20 country singles: "You Win Again," "Right Now," "Going Out Tonight," and the Cajun-tinged "Down at the Twist and Shout." By 1992, Carpenter was picking up the first of two CMA Female Vocalist of the Year awards and the first of five Grammys.

Radio embraced her as well. Her fourth album, *Come On, Come On,* became the biggest of her career, selling more than three million copies and spawning seven Top 20 singles. The album was full of irresistible hooks and poetic imagery. She was a lottery winner choosing between alt-country icons in "I Feel Lucky": "Dwight Yoakam's in the corner, trying to catch my eye / Lyle Lovett's right beside me with his hand upon my thigh." And she was a clear-eyed optimist daring the world to take its best shot in "I Take My Chances":

I've crossed lines of words and wire
And both have cut me deep
I've been frozen out and
I've been on fire
And the tears are mine to weep
But I can cry until I laugh
Or laugh until I cry
So cut the deck right in half
I'll play from either side
I take my chances.

But the song that best epitomized Carpenter's unflinching worldview was "He Thinks He'll Keep Her," a feminist anthem inspired by a 1970s Geritol commercial where a husband compliments his wife's homemaking accomplishments before concluding, "I think I'll keep her." The lyrics depict a woman trapped in a stable but loveless marriage, caught between societal expectations and a need for self-fulfillment and independence.

She does the carpool, she PTAs
Doctors and dentists,
she drives all day
When she was 29
she delivered number three
And every Christmas card
showed a perfect family
Everything runs right on time
Years of practice and design
Spit and polish till it shines
He thinks he'll keep her
Everything is so benign
The safest place you'll ever find
God forbid you change your mind
He thinks he'll keep her.

In another era of country music, the woman might have stood by her man. But Carpenter's heroines never settled. Even when the cost of freedom is a job "in the typing pool at minimum wage." Carpenter was never really a mainstream country artist, but by 1994, she had become a major Nashville star. And "Shut Up and Kiss Me," the first single from her fifth studio album, *Stones in the Road,* continued her commercial appeal, becoming the singer's first No. 1 single.

Oh, baby, when I feel this feeling
It's like genuine voodoo hits me

It's been too long since somebody whispered ...
Shut up and kiss me.

The album also hit No. 1 on the charts, and won Carpenter two Grammys in 1995 — for Best Country Album and Best Country Female Vocal Performance.

But it seemed a turning point as well. Outside of the singles, "Shut Up and Kiss Me" and "Tender When I Want to Be," the album was quiet and introspective, a return to the singer-songwriter's folkier roots. Carpenter had grown older, along with all the 20- and 30-something women she had given voice to.

She married in 2002. Divorced in 2010. Life changed. Music changed. The world changed.

Her 2004 album, *Between Here and Gone,* included the haunting September 11 tribute "Grand Central Station," about an ironworker covered in "holy dust" escorting home the souls of the lost. I was on a train coming into Manhattan when those planes hit the World Trade Center. I watched the smoke pouring out of the buildings into that clear blue sky and, for weeks after they fell, stared each morning at the gray cloud that hovered over lower Manhattan. And in those dark days afterward, my heart shattered every time I walked past those makeshift memorials, where the faces of the missing stared out from walls papered with flyers. The onetime poet of the single woman had taken on heartbreak on a grander scale.

Eventually, Carpenter steered her career away from country, finding a home in folk and Americana and bringing her voice to songs about politics and social issues. Similarly, my own career was growing and expanding, my world enlarging with responsibilities and other interests.

Occasionally I will catch one of her early hits playing on a '90s country station, and I have to smile, remembering the women we both were back then — and how far we both have come.

Carpenter was never just the voice of the single woman. She was the voice of every woman who ever found herself at the corner of love and heartbreak and made a choice, not knowing yet what the future might hold. I'd been at that corner, made my choice, and taken my chances.

I waited. I worked. I built a career, and kept thinking about what the future might hold for my personal life. "I never learned nothing from playing it safe," Carpenter once sang. Nor had I.

Twenty-six years later, I am still living in New York, charting my own course, and, as an editor, pursuing the work that I love. There are still plenty of celebrity interviews and fabulous parties — along with more serious stories that remind me of why I got into journalism in the first place. The days are often long, the deadlines crazy. But when I pour myself into a car after another late-night magazine close, I know I'm doing what I was meant to do.

Carpenter's message was always simple: Be true to yourself and the world will fall into place. Sure, there may be days — or even years — of doubt, but hang on to your dreams. For dreams are the things that light our way.

And somehow, along the way, the rest of my life fell into place as well. In 2011, I met the man I had been looking for all along. One who shares my dreams and passions and treasures the strong and independent woman I've become. We married in 2014, and at the wedding, we danced to Carpenter's 1996 cover of John Lennon's "Grow Old With Me."

Grow old along with me
The best is yet to be ...

The best *was* yet to be. For all of us. ∎

THAT FIRE

Talking with Paula Cole about stardom and womanhood in music

by Kim Ruehl

> ## "I had a very quick ascension, and my five minutes there felt so uncomfortable, like some extremely ill-fitting snake skin that I needed to shed."
> Paula Cole

THE 1990S WAS AN interesting time in music. That final decade of the century, before the internet flipped the recording industry upside down, saw a wide array of styles hitting hard with pop audiences. Radio was dominated equally by divas like Mariah Carey, grunge bands like Nirvana, the very beginnings of an "indie rock" craze (Bush, Live), and hip-hop that was equal parts politically outspoken and sexually provocative. And then there were the woman singer-songwriters.

The year Paula Cole burst onto radio and MTV with her monster hit, "Where Have All the Cowboys Gone" (1996), was the same year Shawn Colvin showed up with "Sunny Came Home," Jewel had "Who Will Save Your Soul," and Joan Osborne delivered "One of Us." There was also Natalie Merchant, Sheryl Crow, Melissa Etheridge, and the list goes on. White ladies with acoustic guitars were suddenly a *thing* in popular music. (Tracy Chapman had been delivering for nearly a decade by that point.)

While the riot grrrls were changing the game in the underground, mainstream labels interested in making a buck off the ensuing wave of feminism started signing up strong, talented women who looked good and could churn out the hits. Cole, an incredibly knowledgeable, highly educated, shape-shifter of a vocalist and songwriter who had a captivating gaze and a bright smile, fit in easily. Her self-produced debut, *This Fire*, scored her the 1998 Best New Artist Grammy Award and a nomination for Best Producer — she didn't win the latter, but was only the third woman ever nominated in the category.

Many of the women in that scene banded together to tour the country with Lilith Fair during the summers of 1997-'99, featuring stars like Cole and festival founder Sarah McLachlan on the main stage even as it launched careers on the smaller side stage, and the industry took notice at the dollar signs that stacked up in its wake. By the end of Lilith Fair's second tour, "female singer-songwriter" was a musical category unto itself. Thus, in its attempt to honor women creators, the music industry began to swing dangerously close to separate-but-equal, as artists like Cole — to-the-core creators, all of them — were expected to remain in tightly defined boxes without pulling in other areas of music that moved them. When Cole dared follow up *This Fire* with a genre-defying effort titled *Amen,* the disc was met with backlash and dud sales. Around the same time, she made the personal decision to focus on her daughter, who had been diagnosed with asthma and was struggling with related health issues even as Cole's marriage was foundering. She divorced her husband and moved back to Massachusetts to be closer to family. Like so many women artists before and since, she shifted her focus from the loud work of performance to the quiet work of mothering.

In the seven and a half years that passed between *Amen* and Cole's third release, *Courage,* the world and the music industry had changed dramatically. Luckily for Cole, music had always been her avenue for navigating such change. Besides, the singer who was inspired by her father's passion for music, who started her performance career at age 17 in front of a big band of swing players, studied jazz at Berklee College of Music, and somehow stumbled into the spotlight for a couple years, never needed the mainstream music industry for validation in the first place.

On her Kickstarter-funded 2017 double-album, *Ballads,* Cole put down her writer's pen to focus on some of the most beloved standards of American music. Among her covers of songs by Bob Dylan and John Coltrane are her interpretations of tunes by Billie Holiday, Sarah Vaughan, Nancy Wilson, Nina Simone, Bobbie Gentry, and others. In a recent interview, which has been edited for clarity, we touched on many of the aforementioned topics, but focused especially on the women who came before her. We started by talking about the balance of motherhood and womanhood with the life of a performer.

KIM RUEHL: Your bio identifies you as "a mother and human being first," which is true about so many women performers. Motherhood requires so much vulnerability and a ceding of control, and soulfulness. I wonder how that all comes through in the music. Is it conscious for you? Or is music your place to put all of that aside and focus on the other parts of you?

PAULA COLE: You know, I feel a kinship with Bobbie Gentry [who I covered on *Ballads*], because she won a Best New Artist Grammy, like me, and she was an introvert, like me, and a self-producer. She didn't get enough acknowledgement for that, which was so rare at the time. She was really turned off by the music business and the patriarchal nature of it, and she retreated to a California valley. I relate so much to that. There have been many, many times that I've wanted to leave this business.

I spoke at [a school, where] I was introduced by the dean of students as "someone who has lived in the seat of the patriarchy in the music business." It was so interesting to be introduced like that because [the music industry] has often felt like a world full of airplane pilots.

I started at Berklee College of Music, which had a 13:1 men-to-women ratio at the time. I was almost always the only female on the van or the plane or the bus, and amongst the crew and the record company. You'd find women in publicity but never behind the recording desk, and very rarely as bandmates. I got used to that and I operated that way. I had friends who were very kind, wonderful men. There are double standards and there's sexism and awful moments … but there are also good moments.

And then you have a child. I was in an awful marriage where the duties weren't shared, it was entirely on me. That's a whole other article in itself. I had somebody's child, and that person was so unlike me in so many ways. I had my beautiful daughter and I was doing everything myself, and still trying to make a living in the music business. It was impossible. It was *completely*

impossible. It required a shutdown of my music career. [My daughter] Sky was sick, she had asthma, I was rotating four meds at a time.

After leaving that situation — divorce, relocating — I came back to my family in Massachusetts. I very much needed my family. I found myself as a single mom trying to make a go of it, still, with my career.

A near-eight-year hiatus is a near-death experience in pop [music]. I was changed personally by what I had gone through, and the world had changed. My former career was pre-internet; my

second career was post-internet. I've been dancing as fast as I can, combining skill sets, as we artists have to do. We have to be entrepreneurial, we have to have emotional intelligence to lead a band. I need to write, [and] I teach now at Berklee College of Music. It's just a lot. I feel for moms, especially single moms. ...

I realized after the making of *Ballads* that I was unconsciously drawn to women's stories. Whether it was Bobbie Gentry in "Ode to Billie Joe," or "Willow Weep for Me," which is one of the rare standards that's written by a woman, Ann Ronell. Even "Naima," by Coltrane,

is about his first wife, who was the wind beneath his wings in a sense. A lot of the smart business decisions he made, like staying with the Miles Davis Quintet, was because of her.

I also have it on my bucket list to support my mother, who did not get to put her art into the world because she was raising us. And my great-grandmother Charlotte was asked to tour with the symphony as a pianist because she was so badass and the family wouldn't let her. It was shameful, it was a Victorian mentality. Joni Mitchell talks about this too. That's part

with them. That's one reason music writers have gotten in the habit of categorizing "female singer-songwriters," which I'm determined to do away with. But how do you navigate that? Is there even time to think about what it means to be a successful woman in this field? It's becoming more normalized now, but certainly in the '90s, when you started, it wasn't normal.

PC: Well, in the '90s there was a lot of music, and a lot of it was good. A lot of it happened to be by females. It was named [by] the Lilith movement, and that became a way to categorize and separate it. It was also good because, especially in the first year of the tour, 1997, [there] was hope. It felt like Woodstock, the audiences were amazing. It felt like a Bernie Sanders rally. ... But in the [process of] categorization, the naming, the corporate sponsorship, it started to separate [from everything else,] so it could start to receive backlash. That was hard to experience. There was greatness in it and also disappointment in it, following [the backlash].

I received a lot of that backlash upon release of my follow-up album, *Amen,* but also for bucking the system and having armpit hair at the Grammys. That was such a big deal to certain people. Jay Leno made a joke out of it, and at the time I didn't find it funny. I was just kind of sick of the music business. And the tide was turning, too, as we were nearing the millennium change, with a bevy of blond singers and Svengali groups run by managers and A&R folks that were matching songs to them, whether it was N*Sync or Backstreet Boys or Christina Aguilera or Britney Spears. They could sing, but they weren't visionary artists, writing. They were very much produced pop and that was the next wave.

Sometimes I'm completely infuriated by a society that view[s] music to be such castoff fashion when it's much more than that. That's why I'm

in it. ... I worship at the altar of music. It's emotional healing, it's therapy, it's the zeitgeist for social change. It heals societies, it heals people. Where you have greater music expression, you have less crime, you have healthier neighborhoods, you have healthier relationships. So it's infuriating to me that artists who are in it — really *in it* — for the truth of it, sometimes they're just whisked away because there's a different age group coming up with a different thing.

I'm also infuriated by Apple Music and Spotify, where, "If you like Paula Cole, you'll like these ten other females." That's ridiculous. That is gender bias in the programming.

KR: I want to go back to Bobbie Gentry. You know, whenever somebody disappears from the music industry for a time, the narrative is always, "Why would you walk away from fame when you can have another record and extend it?" As if life beyond career is irrelevant. Bobbie Gentry did that, and you did it.

PC: For me it felt so good to say no. My psyche was crying out to take a break from it. I had a very quick ascension, and my five minutes there felt so uncomfortable, like some extremely ill-fitting snake skin that I needed to shed [laughs]. I'm an introvert and I'm really into the music and I happen to be very stubborn so I followed it with gusto. I worked hard, with my New England work ethic. And I loved being onstage with my beautiful musicians, whom I had been playing with since I was 19. We were family, so that was all good.

But photo shoots? And feeling objectified? And the commerce of it, and record companies, signing bad deals, being taken advantage of? Incredible. I felt empty, [and also] like Sky was out in the universe somewhere calling me and I needed to have her, like I needed her in the world. ... I knew I needed to share my path with her. She's 15 now and is getting more independent and wears Doc Martens and has purple stripes in

of the reason she moved forward with her career and had to give her daughter up for adoption. She *had* to do this. It's like Carl Jung says: One of the most guiding forces in a lifetime is the unfinished dreams of our parents — and also our grandparents. In this case our mothers and our grandmothers and our great-grandmothers.

KR: With a career such as yours — writer, producer, performer, and all the other levels you have struck — for a woman to have commercial success in all of that is rare. So many women do those things but don't have commercial success

"I realized after the making of 'Ballads' that I was unconsciously drawn to women's stories. Whether it was Bobbie Gentry in 'Ode to Billie Joe,' or 'Willow Weep for Me,' which is one of the rare standards that's written by a woman, Ann Ronell."

Paula Cole

her hair. She is an awesome feminist and I love her so much. She is such an awesome young woman. So hopefully I'll keep walking the path a long time with her.

But increasingly I'm getting to work again, so I'm getting busier now, and [I'm] happy about *Ballads*. It's my first covers album and it shows my roots as a jazz singer and a folk singer. ... It's very different for me. I've always written my own albums.

KR: I wanted to ask you about that. You've said it's the album you've wanted to make for a long time. You've turned down other opportunities to make jazz albums in the past. What is it about this collection, at this time?

PC: I'm very aware of my mortality. I don't know if other people feel it the way I feel it. I have this bucket list. It's always been there, the need to make this album. It's such a mystery, this process of following your muse. ... I just felt that I had written seven albums of content and I didn't need to do that [again]. This was demanding to be done. All I can say is it was in my gut and my psyche. It was gnawing at me. ...

And it was time to rectify the situation of me singing on everybody else's jazz albums. I sung on four Chris Botti albums and a lot of them did well for him. I sang on Terri Lyne Carrington's last album and I'd collaborated with Herbie Hancock. I'd sung on all these soundtracks, jazz

standards. People would say, "You're the best jazz singer that nobody knows about," which is terribly flattering, but ... I needed to make my own vision for it.

I wanted a guitar-based rhythm section. I wanted it to be kind of old-school swinging, like a Muscle Shoals rhythm section that's swinging on jazz. So that's what I did with Kevin Barry on guitar, as the Wes Montgomery of the situation, with his wife, Consuelo Candelaria, who's a brilliant pianist. She's not heard enough because she's the one at home with the kids while Kevin, her husband, is out on tour with Rosanne Cash and all these other people. Consuelo is brilliant and the world hasn't even caught up to that, they haven't even heard her.

KR: True for so many women! But I wonder, as a songwriter, what does it mean to put songwriting aside and dig back into these old songs? The '30s are almost a century ago at this point. There's some kind of connection that happens, across time, between people who are dead now, keeping their voice alive. Can you talk about that?

PC: It was *easy*. I have standards all over my piano and I always have. That's what I play when I'm at home. And I put Ella Fitzgerald on Pandora. That's what I listen to and that's what I study. ...

I was unconsciously drawn to women's voices in the standards, even though they were so rare. Billie Holiday — who I like to describe as one of

America's great singer-songwriters, because she was a songwriter and that was so rare [for women at the time] — "God Bless the Child," that was her song. That's how *Ballads* starts, is with her voice, her reflection of poverty and the hard life she had. She grew up in a whorehouse in Harlem. Her mother took her from Baltimore and was mopping the floors of a whorehouse, and God knows what else. That's how poor Billie Holiday grew up. She wrote that song and it's as relevant today as it was then. [I had to sing] Ann Ronell with "Willow Weep for Me," and Bobbie Gentry with "Ode to Billie Joe."

I've been singing standards since before I started writing my own songs. My first gig was with a big band, a swing band, when I was 17. I was singing jazz through college and learning my dad's music through his fake books and real books, and hearing him play all this music. ... It's all music. I don't like the genres, I don't like the labels.

KR: I'd love to hear you talk about Nina Simone, because she was everything a woman of her time — especially a black woman — was not supposed to be.

PC: What an amazing human being. I feel so sorry for her that she didn't have more support in her life, personally.

I think of her as a gospel and folk singer, and I find it interesting that it's always "jazz, jazz, jazz." What is jazz, anyway? "Jazz" is a word that comes from the brothels of New Orleans, so who knows what that means [laughs].

She was classically trained and played in church, so she has that beautiful gospel style. And look at the songs she covered — so many of them are folk songs. She was so interesting in what she covered, and so prolific in what she covered, and unafraid to speak out. Those artists who speak out about society and justice and politics are the ones who might anger people temporarily, but they are the ones who last. They are the voice for a generation, a society. I say this to my students. I create a social-political playlist and I play Nina Simone and Bob Marley and Crosby, Stills, Nash, & Young and Bob Dylan and Woody Guthrie and Tracy Chapman, and I say, "Is it any coincidence, do you think, that they're not flash-in-the-pans?" They're singing about things that involve all of us, and they have the courage to make their music mean more than their own therapy. It's *collective* therapy.

This is why we need music, and we need it today more than ever. We need "God Bless the Child" more than ever. We need Nina Simone more than ever. We need "The Ballad of Hollis Brown" — you know, [my version of that is] just as much a nod to Nina Simone and her "Sinnerman" style of piano playing as it is to Bob Dylan's lyrics. So Nina Simone — profound, mighty, tempestuous, difficult. Boy do I relate! ∎

An oral history of Trio

by Jonathan Bernstein

A GLORIOUS SOUND

LONG BEFORE THEY BEGAN singing together, Emmylou Harris, Linda Ronstadt, and Dolly Parton had loved each other's music. In fact, Harris once said, "What brought Linda and I together, our first friendship bond, was that Dolly Parton was our favorite singer."

A few years after Ronstadt and Parton met in 1971, the trio recorded some songs together during a mid-'70s session, several of which found their way onto the women's solo albums throughout the ensuing decade.

Linda Ronstadt: "We just loved singing together. It was like, 'Wow, this sounds good, let's do more.'

"When we sang together, it was an unusual sound. It caught our attention. Emmy and I had sung together before, and when we did it with Dolly, when that force was added, it just made it sparkle and jump. Our voices were really different. Dolly's sounds like water skimming over stones, and Emmy's got that cracked crystal quality and it just shimmers. My voice is kind of thick and kind of heavy. So I always thought of it like a candy bar, where you ground everything together."

While those sessions were no doubt satisfying, the women still dreamed of making a full album together. One major thing in their way was the pull of their separate careers.

Dolly Parton (for the 2016 BBC documentary *Sisters in Country: Dolly, Linda, and Emmylou*): "We were all on different labels, we all had different managers, we all were scattered to the wind, all had obligations and tours."

Then, finally, in 1986, Parton, Harris, and Ronstadt found time to commit to a full album, which was recorded throughout the year in a series of sessions helmed by producer George Massenburg. The idea, they all agreed, would be to sing the type of harmony-heavy, old-time mountain music that Parton had grown up with, that Harris had mastered as a performer, and that Ronstadt had always adored.

Herb Pedersen (session banjo player, vocal arranger): "I went out to Linda's place in Malibu with the girls and sat there and listened to their choice of material before they recorded the first album. A lot of the ideas came from Emmy and [musical consultant] John Starling. I wanted to see where the comfort zone was, as far as figuring out which keys they were going to sing the tunes in. We were figuring out who would be best to do this or that and who would be best to sing the baritone or the tenor part."

Linda Ronstadt: "We wanted to sing really straightforward songs that represented our feelings. Emmy and Dolly and I are very attached to singing songs about our feelings and what we're going through at the time in our lives. It's the only motivation for choosing the song.

"Emmy found a lot of the material on the record. She was the best one at coming in with really good songs. So we'd fall in love with them and we'd have to decide who was going to sing lead based on who sounded best, and that was exactly how it was done. It wasn't like, 'I'm going to do it,' 'No, I'm going to do it.' It was, 'I think you should do it.' It was more like that."

Herb Pedersen: "I referred to myself as the vocal referee. When you've got three pretty hardline lead singers and they come together to record, most of the time you'll find that it's hard to determine who's going to sing lead and who's going to sing harmony, because everyone wants to sing lead. But with Dolly, Emmylou, and Linda, they were all bending backward to accommodate each other.

"What I really appreciated about [them] was that they all did their homework. Everybody had their parts nailed down before we'd go into the studio and waste time and money. The keys were picked out, and who was going to sing lead was picked out. Before we even got together, they had already discussed amongst themselves what types of songs they wanted to sing. The music mostly

came from an acoustic format. In other words, it was three girls sitting around in their living room by the fire singing all these old tunes, that kind of thing."

George Massenburg (producer of both *Trio* albums): "It's pretty stunning who played on the *Trio* records, and some of that was hard fought. Getting Ry Cooder to show up was really hard, and once he was there, it was hard to get him to hang around. He'd be walking out the door and we'd have to go coerce him to go back in and do one more take. There were great musicians, just great musicians, on that record. They were very well paid, but for a record of that intensity, you can't be paid enough. ...

"John Starling, my co-producer, was so great to have in the studio because he'd keep me honest. There were moments when we got too far away from bluegrass, and he would arch his eyebrows and just say, 'Are you sure about that?' And I'd ... have to say that I feel good about it and I think the girls feel good about it and I think we're going to have to do it that way if the girls want it. It didn't happen very often, but it did happen occasionally."

Robert Blakeman (photographer): "We had a full day in my studio with the three ladies and we knew we needed to get as much content as we could: the album cover as well as plenty of imagery for publicity and photos inside the album sleeve. In this day and age, it's unlikely you'd ever get three people at that level in the studio at once. They'd

just say, 'Shoot me and put me together in Photoshop.' But this was all of that talent in one place.

"... They all came to my studio separately. I had not yet ever met Dolly, and I remember when she walked in, she's not very tall, probably five foot one, but that height does not speak to her personality and command of the room. She was quite something. She walked right up to me and went, 'God, I am so happy to be here. We're just going to have such fun today.'"

John Kosh (creative director): "Dolly arrived made up in the wig, the whole works, everything."

Linda Ronstadt: "There's a photo of the three of us in white Victorian dresses, where Emmy's holding up a Martin guitar. That guitar belonged to my grandfather. He bought it new, in 1896."

Bob Merlis (publicist, Warner Bros.): "I'll never forget that when they came to the Warner Bros. office around the time the album was released, they walked in the front door and Dolly said to the other two, 'Suck it in, girls!' ...

"The album didn't have a unified theme like *Graceland,* but just having those three together was enough of a story. Albums like that are called 'event albums' nowadays, but we didn't have the term back then. It was really cool that the album was just called *Trio*. It was like, 'We don't have to tell you their names.' It showed that there was an egalitarian spirit in there, an alliance of equals, and

> # "I'll never forget that when they came to the Warner Bros. office around the time the album was released, they walked in the front door and Dolly said to the other two, 'Suck it in, girls.' "
>
> Bob Merlis, Warner Bros. publicist

an alliance of giants. *Trio* was more than the sum of its parts. It reached people in a way that a really great Ronstadt album or a really great Dolly album or a really great Emmylou album maybe wouldn't have. It became its own entity."

Linda Ronstadt: "One of the things *Trio* did was that it brought an awareness of traditional music more into the forefront. At that point, country music was run by these people who would interview fans and say: Do you like a happy song or a sad song? They'd say we like happy songs, and so they'd say to the songwriters: 'Don't bring us any sad songs.'

"But you're not going to write a song if you're happy, you're just going to sit there being happy and enjoy that. Sad songs make you feel happy, as it turns out, because you exorcise that part of your healing that deals with it. The idea that traditional music won't sell has been disproved so many times. Over the years there are always folk scares. I came out of one of the folk scares myself, with Joan Baez and Bob Dylan and Peter, Paul and Mary. People are hungry for traditional music. Ours wasn't strictly traditional, because we had pop stuff too, but we found good pop songs."

An Unexpected Hit

The album came together and finally saw its release in the spring of 1987. Its title told their story in just one word: *Trio.* Yet despite its star power, the commercial viability of the *Trio* album was not a given to many in the industry before its release.

According to Massenburg, the Nashville and Los Angeles divisions of Warner Bros., which released the record, clashed over the album.

Linda Ronstadt: "I don't think anybody liked the idea of three women singers."

Bob Merlis: "When it was revealed that Warner was going to get the *Trio* album, we were so happy. There was a great wellspring of goodwill towards Emmylou at Warner because she had been there for quite a while, and everybody was really excited about having anything to do with Dolly Parton, because she was just so much fun."

Consider that in March of '87, songs like "Mornin' Ride" by Lee Greenwood and "I Can't Win for Losing You" by Earl Thomas Conley — highly-produced, synth-driven '80s ballads — were at the top of the country charts.

But by May of '87, *Trio*'s near a capella, spectral cover of Phil Spector's "To Know Him Is to Love Him" had become, against all odds, the most played song on country radio. By July, just four months after it was released, *Trio* had sold over one million copies. The album topped the country albums chart for five weeks and became a Top Ten hit on the pop charts. It went on to sell more than four million copies, spawn several successful singles, win a variety of country music industry awards, and even garner a Grammy nomination for Album of the Year alongside Prince, Michael Jackson, U2,

and Whitney Houston in 1988.

George Massenburg: "It hit Nashville like a bomb. They loathed it.

"We were not popular for making this record. Nashville did not like the fact that we were doing this record. We did it out of Warner's in California and not Warner's in Nashville, and there were a lot of hard feelings. Nashville hated it, talked it down, bad-mouthed it, and then tried to copy it as best as they could.

"... The key thing about *Trio* is that it's the story of three very strong artists doing exactly what they wanted to do and who weren't going to be pushed around by a record company. That's kind of the whole story."

In retrospect, the historically minded, deeply reverent approach to traditional American music on *Trio,* radical at the time for three pop stars as successful as Harris, Ronstadt, and Parton, became the standard for what has since become called Americana music. Its success set the tone, a decade or so later, for the monumental roots-music explosion that came with *O Brother, Where Art Thou?* at the turn of the century.

George Massenburg: "The success surprised everybody. It opened up a tremendous opportunity for other artists to work in that format and genre, to work in bluegrass. Mary Chapin Carpenter and Randy Travis, although he's hardly bluegrass, came shortly thereafter. New Grass Revival came together, and what also emerged from *Trio* was an

the people on the business side prevailed."

Jim Keltner (session drummer): "As far as I can remember, Dolly was not there at the studio and there was some situation that they had going on between them that caused her not to be there. It seemed like they were a little annoyed that she wasn't able to be there. I think she had overbooked herself and couldn't be there, but it all worked out good."

George Massenburg: "Here's what happened: At the last minute Dolly went to do something else. There were some misunderstandings but we're all pretty much over that stuff. Everything has been kind of forgiven and forgotten."

Linda Ronstadt: "Scheduling was impossible. Managers and agents always want to do what's going to make them the most money, and putting the three of us on the road when we'd have to split it three ways wasn't going to make us the most money. I didn't even think of it that way. The three of us on the road would have been a really musical time. We would have spent all our evenings in a room together, just jamming. With that bunch of musicians and that assemblage of voices, that would have been really fun. But it just couldn't have happened. It was just impossible. Apart from television, we were only on stage once, when Dolly and I sat in at one of Emmy's shows."

The sequel was a slightly more modern take on the same collection of bluegrass-indebted source material, included stunning covers of Neil Young's "After the Gold Rush" and Parton's "Do I Ever Cross Your Mind." *Trio II* was also a success, though not quite as much of a blockbuster as their debut. Still, it was certified gold, earned a Grammy nomination for Best Country Album, and reached the Top Ten on the country charts.

Jim Keltner: "The *Trio II* record for me was a standout. It was a really good gig because those girls are amazing, and that particular time, they were on the top

opportunity for Alison Krauss. It all came out of Linda and Emmy and to a certain extent, Dolly's vision. Linda and Emmy especially, a little less so Dolly, because she's very commercial-minded."

Bob Merlis: "It was the most amazing thing when 'To Know Him Is to Love Him' won a BMI award that year. Phil Spector went and accepted the award in Nashville. It really underscores how ecumenical that project was. Dolly, she's a country singer. Emmylou was Americana if they had the term back then, and Ronstadt was a rock and pop singer. And then country radio embraced the record. I remember seeing a picture of Spector with that award and thinking, 'Man, this is the least obvious thing you can imagine.'"

It Got Complicated

It was more than a decade before the group managed to release their follow-up album, *Trio II,* which had been recorded years earlier, in the mid-'90s, but like its predecessor was delayed and backlogged due to conflicting schedules and obligations.

Linda Ronstadt: "It got very complicated, finding a time to record and put out the albums. You don't want to have a *Trio* record coming out when you're putting out your solo record, because it means you're competing with yourself. I didn't care about any of that stuff, I mainly just cared about the music, and [we all] felt the same way. But

of their game. As far as I'm concerned, there's nobody with a voice like Linda Ronstadt. Emmylou was otherworldly, and then Dolly is amazing, just incredible. As a drummer, I play to the vocal in the studio, which is a big no-no, but I could never seem to get away from doing that. So getting to play with singers like that was such a great lesson for me, and so much fun."

George Massenburg: "It's my strongest feeling that recording live in the studio, where everybody hears each other and can respond to what they hear in the moment, is best. There's a great thing that happens as musicians respond to one another: They build a musical story and it's a common story. The few times that we had to overdub it was a real struggle, because you don't know whose vocals should go on first. Usually Emmy sang low, Linda middle, and Dolly high, but it wasn't always that way for all of the harmonies, a lot of times there was crossover that we didn't anticipate.

"There was a lot of back and forth between Nashville and Los Angeles, just to get a few finishing touches on the last songs. It's much better off if you can just hear everything at the same time in the same place, where all the artists can agree on tempos and keys."

Linda Ronstadt: "We had to overdub vocals because there would always be something that'd be mis-phrased when we sang live. We worked on the harmonies as we went. Our voices fit together in an unusually good way, but we didn't have the pleasure and the advantage of spending hours and hours on the bus because we didn't tour together, so we didn't have a lot of time to work out our vocals and our harmonies and get used to each other's pitch centers and how to sing with each other, so we had to spend a lot of time in the studio getting it right.

"Dolly didn't like to spend a lot of time in the studio. I lived for the studio. I could sit in there for 15 hours and not get bored. So it was hard for us to understand that about each other sometimes. I'd want to keep doing it until it was perfect. But we worked on it hard enough without killing each other."

Like Sisters

In 2016, to round out the trio's run with a third release, Rhino Records released *The Complete Trio Collection*, a three-album collection compiling the group's first two albums alongside 20 alternate takes and unreleased demos, capping off the historic group's recording archive roughly 40 years after they began singing together.

James Austin (co-producer of *The Complete Trio Collection*): "It took about ten years to tie up all the loose ends for this project because with three people, the process is going to take three times as long, because you have to make sure everyone feels like they've been included. Emmylou [co-producer of the compilation] would always say, 'Let's check with Linda, let's check with Dolly.' That spirit of inclusion was really beautiful. It was always 'we,' it was never 'I.'"

Herb Pedersen: "Oh my god, they love each other, and you could just tell from the get-go when we first went to the studio."

Bob Merlis: "They all really admired each other, and it wasn't contrived. Sometimes, somebody guests on an album and it gets your attention, but that's about it. But this wasn't a marketing concept. It was something that three artists of equivalent stature decided that they wanted to do because they really liked each other, and it worked because they could hear it. You could hear their mutual respect. All three of them were really perfectionists, and they all did great work. Together, they did even greater work."

James Austin: "The level of cooperation and love and mutual respect that they have for each other is the one thing that probably overrides everything that I've gone through. That's the thing that I took away from this experience the most: the idea that no one was playing the superstar in that group. They're like sisters. The word 'sisters' is really appropriate."

Linda Ronstadt: "When I think of *Trio*, I think of 'My Dear Companion.' That's the one. That song starts with Emmy singing, and then I join in, and then you hear what we sound like as a duet. And then Dolly comes in and you hear what the trio sounds like. It's all of the components and then eventually the whole thing. It was a perfect vehicle for us.

"We liked to think of our songs as parlor music, songs a housewife would sing, or even people in the country. They had very little leisure time but maybe when they finished with all their chores they'd sit down together and play a song. We thought of our music as parlor music, ladylike. Or maybe you'd be singing them all by yourself. That kind of parlor music seems to be going out of style.

"Now, we delegate our singing and dancing and visual art to professionals and we just observe and become very passive participants in art. But we should be *making* art. You don't have to show it to anybody. No need to overshare. But it's important for people to know singing and dancing. That's what *Trio* was supposed to do. ...

"What I really remember is just sitting in a living room, either mine or Dolly's, and just working out the harmony parts. That was just pure joy. You hear a song and you'll go, 'Oh that'll work, I'll sing this and you sing that.' And we'd try it the other way around, and when we hit the right combination, it was just so fun. It was very satisfying, musically.

"I grew up singing with my brother and sister and we had a natural blend, and I had always missed that. Playing in a band, you sing harmony with whoever's playing with you, and that'd change over the years with different band members. But when we heard that vocal combination, of me, Dolly, and Emmy, it was the first time that I really felt like I had something that was like what I had with my brother and sister."

Emmylou Harris (for *Sisters in Country: Dolly, Linda, and Emmylou*): "It was a glorious sound." ■

Emmylou Harris and Daniel Lanois performing the entirety of *Wrecking Ball* in Nashville in 2012.

SEEING INTO THE FUTURE

Talking with Daniel Lanois about Emmylou Harris' 'Wrecking Ball'

by Stephen Deusner

GROWING UP IN QUEBEC IN the 1960s, Daniel Lanois always had a fascination with American music, with the sounds and rhythms and mythologies of the American greats. He took a circuitous route to work with them: graduating from a neighborhood studio gig to a series of collaborative ambient albums with Brian Eno to a co-production gig with U2 that lasted longer than that band's relevance. Along the way he developed an idiosyncratic sound, one based in ambient texture but still emphasizing rhythm and the particularities of the human voice, which made him a surprisingly good match as a producer for Emmylou Harris.

Lanois brought all of that to bear with Harris's 1995 album *Wrecking Ball*, which at the time seemed like an outlier in her catalog: Rather than the stately twang that had defined her music since her earliest duets with Gram Parsons in the late 1960s, these songs shimmer and wobble, a memory of American music coalescing into something strange and inviting — not country, but not *not* country either. The parts are familiar, in other words, but the whole is new. Especially coming one year after Johnny Cash's *American Recordings*, *Wrecking*

Ball suggested a resurgence of country veterans taking more risks than the youngsters who had displaced them.

More than even Cash's comeback, however, *Wrecking Ball* has much in common with Lanois' subsequent albums — specifically, Bob Dylan's *Time Out of Mind* in 1997 and Willie Nelson's *Teatro* in 1998. Together, these three discs stand as a loose yet monumental Americana trilogy: All are standouts from late in these artists' careers, of course, but also they all reimagine traditional American music for the pre-millennial moment, acting together to point in a direction roots music was poised to take in the new century, at least until *O Brother, Where Art Thou?* popularized a much more literal, re-creative approach.

"It was not planned," says Lanois. "I didn't mean to work with those three particular artists in that short period of time. Now that I look back, it does seem pretty short. It just happened. How lucky is it that a Canadian kid would get to work with three American treasures a few years apart like that? And French Canadian on top of that."

I recently spoke with Lanois about all three of these albums. Part I is below, focusing on *Wrecking Ball*, Harris' home, and Lanois' attempts to create a new

sound for her. Parts II and III — about *Time Out of Mind* and *Teatro* — will appear in the next *No Depression* journal.

STEPHEN DEUSNER: Why did you want to work with Emmylou?

DANIEL LANOIS: I was always fascinated with the South, so when I had a chance to work with a woman from Alabama, my first thought was: "Okay, I'm going to learn something here."

Obviously, her having sung with so many of the greats had a lot to do with the decision, but when I met her in Nashville and visited her home, I felt there was a lot of dignity in her house of American values. I was very struck by the wonderful values she was operating by. It was so nice to be in that house, and that's largely why I said yes.

Funny, she's obviously one of the great American singers, and I knew that before I went in, but when I felt the vibrations in that house, I thought, "Okay, this is something I never grew up with."

I come from a broken home, drifting around a lot, so to be in a house of stability and dignity really meant a lot to me.

SD: Did you consider recording at her home, to get the vibe off the place?

DL: No, I didn't think about recording in her house. It's a very domestic place.

"She'd done bluegrass, and she'd done classic country, but I saw another dimension of country music or roots music in her work. I felt a responsibility to go to that dimension so that we weren't just going up a familiar road."

Daniel Lanois

Her mom was in there and her kids. It really felt like a home. Emmy always had her little songwriting room, but I thought that belonged to her in a very private way.

We had a band together, drums and everything. We needed a place where we could make a bit of a racket, and I didn't want to rattle those beautiful photographs that were on her mantle. I didn't think it was right to record in her house — although I thought about it in a different way. If I worked with her again, I thought I might choose to bring some pre-made recordings for her to overdub onto. That could happen in her house, and she might appreciate not being too far away from her kitchen.

SD: How did you prepare for these sessions? Did you have an idea of how the album would sound, or was it more of an exploratory project?

DL: I didn't have a lot of preconceptions. She sent a cassette of three or four songs, just her solo. I think she made them at home, and they were very beautiful and stark. I thought that singularity should be held onto even with the framing —

framing the picture with more musicians. I didn't want to lose that center.

I think that's what all [three] of those records have in common: They have very strong centers. Even though we had a full, large band around Dylan, his voice commands the picture, and same with Willie Nelson. That's when you're dealing with artists of that caliber, you don't want to suffocate them in a bunch of production ideas, which is the crime in our line of work — suffocating somebody to the point where it's not even them anymore. I wouldn't want to do that to these people.

SD: This album marks such a departure for Emmylou. Did you have to convince her to take this leap?

DL: When I visited her house, I realized that she was a very broad-minded person and that maybe she hadn't stretched outside of her familiar territory. She'd done bluegrass, and she'd done classic country, but I saw another dimension of country music or roots music in her work. I felt a responsibility to go to that dimension so that we weren't just going up a familiar road.

SD: She does so many beautiful covers on the album — Steve Earle's "Goodbye," Neil Young's "Wrecking Ball," the McGarrigle Sisters' "Goin' Back to Harlan" — but the Jimi Hendrix song "May This Be Love" stands out.

DL: I always thought Jimi Hendrix was a great country guitar player, and that guitar playing style shows up on titles like "Little Wing" and "May This Be Love." There's even a film of him playing an acoustic 12-string — not the electrified [guitar] — and you can really hear his command of the instrument. That always lived in the back of my mind, so when I went to see Emmy, I thought, "Well, it might be nice to visit that part of American sound. It would be unexpected for Emmylou."

SD: What were the sessions at Woodland Studios in Nashville like?

DL: We recorded at Woodland because it's just a very nice, plain, large room, like a BBC orchestral room. That's where we hit upon that sound. I rented an upright piano that had a really good sound to it. Emmy had some dulcimers in her house, laptop dulcimers with double strings, two unison strings per note. Then I had my Martin 12-string with a pickup on it, and my little Vox IX guitar, which is kind of a little mini 12-string. All those instruments had that in common: that a given note has more than one string.

We started working with these instruments, and we hit on a sound pretty early on at Woodland. It reminded me of some of the great sounds that I loved on Phil Spector records — early '60s girl groups that he was producing — the Crystals, for example. I always loved, "He walked up to me, and he asked me if I wanted to dance, da-da-da-da." It was something really fantastic about that sound.

SD: What made that sound so compelling for her?

DL: When I heard the sound, I realized, "Okay, that's what it is. It's a combination of those string instruments ringing." I was thankful that the direction had been laid out for us. I ran into the control room, and I said to Malcolm Burn, who was engineering at the time, "Please don't change anything. Let's leave everything exactly as-is, and I want to study what we

have so that I can continue with the sound that we hit on."

These might be regarded as subtleties by somebody else, but in the middle of work they're very important to me. A flavor presents itself that suggests that this record could be unique.

And that's it.

When I heard that sound, I knew we had something special, and I just stuck with it. It didn't matter if we had drums and bass; the heart of the matter would be those string instruments, these acoustic instruments. Any symphonics that you hear on that record were made with those instruments. We didn't overdub strings, or use keyboards much at all, I don't think. That's it. We found a way to bring traditional American instruments into the future at that moment, even if it meant revisiting the past with Phil Spector.

[On *Wrecking Ball*,] she is drawing from tradition, but also seeing into the future. I thank my lucky stars that we hit on it early on, because taking a traditional form and a singer who has operated within that form and seeing into the future — that's not easy to do. ■

she come by it natural

Part Three:

During a cultural window for female empowerment in the 1980s, Dolly Parton becomes the boss

This is the third installment in a four-part series by our No Depression Writing Fellow, Sarah Smarsh. She is spending 2017 writing about Dolly Parton. Read the final installment in the Winter 2017 issue of this journal.

By Sarah Smarsh

In the 1980 movie *Nine to Five*, three fed-up women take on the male boss who berates, gropes, and demeans them. A parable imparting lessons for men and women alike, the movie was for many viewers the first articulation and condemnation of flagrantly, dangerously sexist office culture that had long been accepted as "the way things are" or "boys being boys."

For Dolly Parton, playing the boss's objectified secretary wasn't a stretch. Just a few years prior, she had quit *The Porter Wagoner Show*, where she had spent years on the payroll of one of Nashville's most infamous male egos.

"I know all about bosses from Porter Wagoner," Parton told *Entertainment Weekly* in 2009, after writing the score for *Nine to Five*'s Broadway adaptation. "He was a male chauvinist pig too."

Perhaps that is why, of the three powerhouse female leads — Parton, Jane Fonda, and Lily Tomlin — the least accomplished actress gives, for my money, the most convincing portrayal.

Fonda and Tomlin knew sexism, of course. And Tomlin, the daughter of a factory worker who — as Parton's father briefly did — left an impoverished life in the South for steady work in Detroit, surely knew firsthand the intersections of gender and economic strife. But something sparkles about Parton onscreen, in particular, and it's not just her frosted eye shadow.

It's that she was entering the apex of her career — a period in which she would become not just a movie star but a major business developer and a global pop culture icon. She would do it all in a huge platinum-blond wig and rhinestone-encrusted spandex, sporting the sort of cleavage that good feminists back then might not have approved of. She didn't give a shit; Parton was beholden to herself and her own desires rather than to a prescriptive cause.

She was, perhaps, a third-wave feminist born a generation early, simultaneously defying gender norms and reveling in gender performance before that was a political act. Country girls like me — in places feminist polemics don't tend to reach — were

watching.

I recently attended a screening of *Nine to Five* in an Austin, Texas, theater full of women shouting at the screen. People think of the film as a comedy, and that's how I had remembered it from TV airings when I was a kid. But rewatching it as a grown woman, I felt a wave of trauma-triggered nausea overcome me when Parton's character is physically grabbed by her boss. I heard women in the audience cheer when the lead characters fantasize about murder and laugh when they roll what they think is their boss's dead body into the trunk of a car. I realized it is one of the darkest movies ever made about the female experience.

It is also, still, painfully relevant. Thirty-six years after the film's release, the US presidency is occupied by a man who embodies the disgusting male boss. Starring in a reality show in which he got off on delivering the words "you're fired," Donald Trump infamously told a female contestant she would look good on her knees. Contestants in the beauty pageants he owned have reported that he had a habit of walking in while they were changing clothes. In these times, *Nine to Five* feels so radical that one wonders whether it would be greenlighted by a major studio today.

Born the same year *Nine to Five* was released, I am now about the age that Parton was when she starred in the film. I also happen to be what during my 1980s childhood and 1990s adolescence people still called "a professional woman" — financially independent since age 18 by the sweat of my own brow, happily divorced and childless, more driven by career goals than domestic ones.

I have come to think of myself and similar women of my generation as *Nine to Five*'s cultural offspring. We formed in a confusing cultural soup of new social freedoms and old expectations. Society was embracing a new vision of the modern woman: She left in the morning to work as a doctor, an engineer, a police officer. But did she also like to bake? Of course, it's possible to love to cook, wear high heels, and do all manner of stereotypically "feminine" things and be no less a feminist for it. Mainstream

culture seems to be clear on that today. But the defining friction for women in the late 20th century was to be newly encouraged to become whatever they wanted, even as they were criticized no matter how they went about it. If they charged into the male-dominated halls of business or government, their feminism made them shrill Amazons in the eyes of threatened men; if they wore low-cut shirts and tight pants while making empowered decisions, their feminism was missed altogether in the eyes of threatened women.

The idea of gender equality both at home and at work was so new then that a woman's entire life could be experienced as an intentional corrective for stereotypes and unfair treatment for her gender. A little more than a decade after *Nine to Five*'s release, in 1992, the first lady of Arkansas — a Yale Law School-educated attorney named Hillary Clinton — caught hell for telling reporters covering her husband's presidential campaign why she worked on public policy rather than draperies as the wife of a governor.

"I suppose I could have stayed home and baked cookies and had teas," Clinton said. "But what I decided to do was to fulfill my profession, which I entered before my husband was in public life." That quote, and widespread pearl-clutching in response to it, would continue to haunt her 24 years later when she ran for president herself.

Clinton spoke snidely about baking cookies not because she hates to bake but because for centuries society has handed women aprons while begrudging them social and political power. Similarly, Parton fashioned herself as a "floozy" not because she sought men's sexual approval but because she stood in solidarity with poor, invisible women whose only hope for survival is through their sex.

In the herky-jerky social gains that unfolded at the end of the last century, women had no choice but for their actions to be reactions. It is a conundrum inherent to any sort of disadvantage, if one means to fight it. In *Nine to Five*, the female leads aren't homicidal criminals by nature. They don't *want* to kill their

"I know all about bosses from Porter Wagoner," Parton told *Entertainment Weekly* in 2009, after writing the score for *Nine to Five*'s Broadway adaptation. "He was a male chauvinist pig too."

boss. But they find that perhaps they must.

According to original screenwriter Patricia Resnick, her first version of the script had to be reframed in order to be produced. In a 2015 interview with *Rolling Stone* marking the movie's 35th anniversary, Resnick said she had wanted to make "a very dark comedy in which the secretaries actually tried to kill the boss." Those plot points were rewritten as fantasy sequences in the interest of the three protagonists' likability.

As for general casting, that the lead actresses would all be white probably wasn't even questioned. A woman of color rarely headlines a film to this day, much less as a protagonist pointing a gun at a white male boss.

Something else that hasn't changed is the relevance of the gender points the movie managed to make. Resnick recalled conversations with skeptical media when the movie was turned into a Broadway production in 2009.

"It was really frustrating," she said, "because a lot of the interviews that I did with male journalists, the first thing they said was, 'Well, none of those issues are a problem in contemporary life, so how are women of today going to be able to relate to it?' I thought, yeah, you can't sexually harass someone as obviously. We don't call people 'secretaries.' Other than that, what has changed?"

As a woman who has held many jobs in the workforce over the course of more than 20 years and never — not once — worked somewhere without some sort of harassment or other poor treatment for my gender, I must say that I agree. The relentless emotional drain of being dismissed, underpaid, ogled, and perceived as a threat is no small part of why I now sacrifice the many benefits and securities of organizational employment in order to work as a self-employed writer.

What's different for me and my generation than it was for our mothers and grandmothers, as Resnick articulates, is that many of the men who have

antagonized us in workplaces did so in ways much quieter than *Nine to Five*'s bombastic chauvinism — often while purporting to be "feminists." That can be an even more dangerous professional climate for women; insidious misogyny or sexism can cut you before you see it and is the hardest to prove.

Feminism and all movements for social progress inevitably contain a gap between what's on paper and what's really going on: between the feminism proclaimed and the feminism enacted, the women's rights legislated and the women's rights enforced, the progress in policy and the progress in culture. Women of Generation X, of which I represent the youngest contingent, had more freedom than their mothers in meaningful ways. We were the first full beneficiaries of Title IX protections guaranteeing access to education and outlawing sexual discrimination in the workplace. We were entering our first romantic partnerships as the Violence Against Women Act became law. But the cultural cues we received growing up were full of gaps and dissonance.

I was recently stunned by an old episode of *Moonlighting*, a favorite childhood show that in my memory was a feminist triumph for featuring Cybill Shepherd as a whip-smart (and damn funny) detective. Bruce Willis' character, the smirking work partner with whom she has just ended an on-again-off-again romance, appears in her house against her will. He refuses to leave when she tells him to, slaps her in the face for arguing with him — and then is welcomed into her arms for his relentlessness.

My 20th century child eyes had seen a strong woman putting up a fight and then being turned on by a man persistent enough to win. But my 21st century adult eyes saw a dangerously entitled man stalking a woman and refusing to respect or even believe her when she said "no."

That was the confusion *Nine to Five* articulated at the start of that decade: a woman's new role in the economy at

cross purposes, in men's eyes, with her old role in bed. Female Baby Boomers faced it, and their Generation X daughters watched them come home ragged in high heels and with little time or awareness to complain.

To be sure, those same woes affect women today and will do so for generations to come. But *Nine to Five* represents a specific moment of tension in feminism's evolution: The Equal Rights Amendment hadn't yet been squashed, middle-class women were power-walking to work (as poor women had been doing all along, by the way), and popular culture revealed a deep collective crisis about the roles of men and women.

That decade of transition — from the Carter era to the Reagan, from polyester bell bottoms to stone-washed denim, from women's-lib signs to the incorrect presumption that liberation had occurred — marked an epic shift in Parton's career, too. Having established herself as a solo country-music star as a young woman in the 1970s, *Nine to Five* turned her into a mainstream Hollywood superstar and accelerated her toward becoming a cultural icon.

Parton never leveraged her celebrity at podiums in feminist marches or in overt political action. But she did choose as her first script, among what must have been ample options, a movie conceived by one of the most vilified feminists of the time — Jane Fonda, then still a divisive figure with her anti-war "Hanoi Jane" controversy fresh in national memory. And Parton accepted as her first role a character who lassoes her abusive boss and shoves a pistol in his face.

Surely it's no accident that Parton was eager to play Doralee, the pretty secretary both sexually harassed and assaulted by her repugnant male boss and ostracized by her female co-workers, who spread the false rumor that she was sleeping with him.

Doralee's particular affliction among the other mistreated female workers was being deemed a "slut" because of her sexy appearance and other men's false claims that they were banging her. Parton herself got used to that in high school.

"I wore a lot of makeup. I wore real tight clothes, and I wore my hair a mile high. I looked like the real trash that a lot of the girls were," Parton told David Letterman on the *Late Show* in 1987. "A lot of those people thought I was a bad influence on their daughters 'cause I told jokes and I wore a lot of makeup. Actually I was pretty good. I just had a real outgoing personality. Some of the girls I was hanging around with were really doing it, and I was gettin' all the credit for it."

Feminist Sweet Spot

I sometimes feel fortunate to have come of age during the feminist sweet spot after the organized marches and policy triumphs of the 1970s but before the full-throated conservative backlash of the new millennium. After *Roe v. Wade* but before conservative zealots created a successful policy strategy for chipping away at reproductive rights. After women entered traditionally male occupations en masse but before technology was harnessed by internet trolls to stalk, harass, and shame them. After female journalists began hosting national network shows but before Fox News put their legs in the shot.

Women my age — children and adolescents in the '80s, teenagers and young women in the '90s — may remember that time more through its records, cassette tapes, and television dials than for its adult politics. But what we found through those albums and TV series often had a decidedly political undercurrent.

Our most formative years came before the hot-pink, baby-talk girl power of the Spice Girls and Britney Spears and the overt, unapologetic embrace of the term "feminism" by Beyoncé and the Dixie Chicks. We

had instead a slew of tough bitches in pantsuits, running intellectual circles around the men they worked with: Murphy Brown, Dana Scully. In big, angular hairdos, delivering the nightly news: Connie Chung, Diane Sawyer. In heels on their way out the door as elegant but take-no-crap working moms: Clair Huxtable, Angela Bower. In leather jackets, singing pop songs in which they embodied a street-wise sexual power: Whitney Houston, Selena. In baggy pants and sneakers, rapping demands for respect: Queen Latifah, Salt-n-Pepa. And in combat boots telling the world to absolutely fuck off: Shirley Manson, Sinéad O'Connor.

As for pop-country music, a genre increasingly associated with conservativism, that period featured women in rhinestones and fringed leather singing triumphantly about hard-won independence.

In her 1986 hit "Little Rock," Reba McEntire decides her marriage to an affluent businessman isn't worth a loveless life and slips off her wedding band: "He never calls me honey / but he sure loves his money."

In their first single, "(That's What You Do) When You're in Love," from their 1985 self-titled album, the Forester Sisters tell a distraught husband confessing the morning after he slept with someone else not to worry because, heck, they've wanted to cheat, too.

He expected me to cry

and hang up the phone...
He said you're some kind of woman
to feel this way
'Cause honey, I expected
there'd be hell to pay...
I said I know that you think
I'm being kind and sweet
But loneliness can be a
two-way street.
Many times I've had to fight
the urge to cheat.
I'm just sayin' that I understand.
As he stood there thinkin'
'bout the words I said
I think he began to see.

It ain't your grandma's "Stand By Your Man."

In another catchy song my mom played over and over in the tape deck of her car, this one from 1987, K.T. Oslin declares that she has started entertaining younger lovers:

Women peak at 40,
and men at 19.
I remember laughing my head off
when I read that in a magazine
(I was 20 at the time).
Now I'm staring 40 right in the face,
And the only trouble with being a
woman my age, is the men my age.

My mom was only in her mid-20s herself when that single hit radio airwaves, and I was all of seven. But, as Mom cruised down the road with a Marlboro Light between her fingers

Parton in the role of Doralee in *Nine to Five*.

and I bobbed my head in the passenger seat, we both relished talking along with the song's spoken aside. Oslin herself is behind the wheel, flipping the usual gender roles of cat-caller in the vehicle and cat-callee on the sidewalk:

Whoa, look over here.
We got a cute little ol' runner
to the right.
Blue shorts, no shirt.
WOOOO! You're lookin' good, darlin'!
That's right — stay in shape.

Once we were singing that song when, my hand to God, we drove past a man jogging in blue shorts, and we both cracked up — a blissful surge of empowerment coursing through us from Oslin's songwriting pen to a busted road in Kansas. I'm not sure how either of us resonated with the particular power reversal inherent to a middle-aged woman singing those words, but a 20-something mom and her precocious daughter somehow already understood.

Parton was middle-aged by then, too, and had been ahead of the times in writing songs about sexual power. As the 1970s wound down, she began shifting her lyrics away from the broken, wronged women her earlier career documented to up-tempo songs like the pop-country hit "Two Doors Down" from the disco-inflected 1978 album *Here You Come Again.*

In the song, the woman singing has dumped her boyfriend but isn't inclined to mope around about the ordeal. She hears a rager going on down the hallway and moseys in that direction: "I think I'll dry these useless tears and get myself together/ I think I'll wander down the hall and have a look around." It's sung sweetly and seems innocent enough. By the next verse, though, she's asking a man from the party to come to her place.

I can't believe I'm standing here
dry-eyed, all smiles and talkin'.
Makin' conversation
with the new love I have found.
I ask him if he'd like to be alone,
and we start walkin'.
Down the hall to my place
waitin' two doors down.

Parton, who made a home in Los Angeles in 1976, surely was influenced by the sexual liberation messages of that period's counter-culture movement. But she has described feeling that same freedom and power as a teenager in rural Tennessee — self-possession before society approved.

Having married soon after arriving in Nashville at age 18 in 1964, the extent to which Parton's sexual experience has or hasn't remained in the province of monogamous marriage is for her to know. ("I said I was married," she told *The New York Times* in 2016. "I didn't say I was dead.") But the garish 1980s saw her exaggerating her appearance in new ways that suggest a woman truly coming into her own, sexually. The deep cleavage now synonymous with her image appeared in that decade — her costumes as Porter Wagoner's duet partner had been high-necked and demure, if sparkly. So too in the '80s emerged her proclivity for defending women whom society might cast as tramps and whores, whether in the personal style she honed or in the movie roles she chose to accept.

After portraying misunderstood, slut-shamed Doralee in *Nine to Five,* in 1982 Parton starred alongside Burt Reynolds as the quintessential heart-of-gold prostitute in *The Best Little Whorehouse in Texas.* It's worth noting that in the brothel she's no longer a worker bee but rather the queen. Not the one being turned out but the one doing the turning. But the metaphor of the downtrodden working girl is one that would always inflect her worldview.

"When I think somebody's acting more like a pimp than a manager, and I'm more of a prostitute than an artist, I always tell them where to put it," Parton told *Maclean's* in 2014. "People will use you as long as you let them."

The feminism inherent in Parton's music and persona might have been lost on cultural critics of the day, but behind the scenes it was hard to miss. While in Austin the year *Best Little Whorehouse* was released, Parton asked to meet firebrand Texas liberal Ann Richards, who was making her first run for state treasurer.

When they met at the storied Driskill Hotel in downtown Austin, photographer Scott Newman was shooting a campaign event for Richards. He snapped a photograph of the women standing together: Richards, a progressive known for flagrant feminism and terrific one-liners, and Parton, a new movie star known for her version of the same thing.

In the black-and-white photo, the two women are in profile, overwhelmed with joyful laughter and near mirror images but for difference in age and body shape — blond, tight curls atop both their heads and ruffles on both their tops.

"What a scene to witness!" Newman wrote in the notes for a recent exhibition of his photography. "These two women, two of my all-time favorite human beings, took such delight in each other."

Parton and Richards would become great friends and were both on their way up: Parton to becoming a pop culture icon and Richards to becoming, as of this writing, the last woman and the last Democrat to govern the state of Texas. Two different paths, but two women with much in common.

The Lone Star State, as well as country music and indeed the entire country, has changed a lot in the more than three decades since that picture was taken. Texas and the rest of the country has swung right; one doubts Ann Richards would win a Texas race today. Meanwhile, Nashville has shunned female political renegades like the Dixie Chicks while embracing a slew of male stars, from "bro country" Luke Bryan to old-school, bearded outlaw Chris Stapleton. Country radio stopped playing Parton's new music decades ago. It's hard to imagine the Southern Gothic defenses of poor women she penned in her 20s making it on the air today.

But there in that 1982 photograph, in a Southern state capital, is the brief but powerful juncture in American history that girls like me — then a toddler living in a metal trailer on the Kansas prairie — somehow absorbed. A female politician and a female country-superstar-gone-Hollywood, exchanging looks of mutual respect and delight, throwing back their heads and laughing in the public space of power that reactionary 21st-century misogyny had not yet spread its male legs to reclaim.

Body Politics

Parton dared to exaggerate her physical features in a way some feminists of her generation might have frowned upon, but she was so objectified and coveted from the start — back when every part of her body was "real" — I'm not sure she had much choice in carrying a hyper-awareness of her form and its relationship to the world. Every woman suffers under the male gaze, but Parton's experience reveals how invisible a woman's humanity might be rendered when that gaze is a laser beam the size of Earth.

When she went on *The Tonight Show* in 1977, Johnny Carson, whose persona was something of a gentleman, stammered and said, "I have certain guidelines on this show, but I would give about a year's pay to peek under [her top]."

She couldn't even escape being made a visual object by a blind man. In 1978, at the awards show where she became the second woman ever to be named the Country Music Association Entertainer of the Year (now one of seven, total), visually impaired singer Ronnie Milsap told the crowd, "I want to know why she wasn't in my braille *Playboy*." (Parton had appeared on the cover of that month's issue of the magazine in a bunny outfit but had refused to pose nude.)

In her 1994 autobiography, *Dolly: My Life and Other Unfinished Business,* Parton describes the pressures she faced during that time without pointing out or perhaps completely realizing the gendered component to all of them: male business associates with bad advice, her siblings' resentment for her fame and fortune in spite of her undeniable generosity as a maternal caretaker, Hollywood's sexist body-shaming.

The shoot for *Best Little Whorehouse* was particularly miserable, Parton writes, citing the set's generally bad vibe. Her small but voluptuous shape was considered fat for the big screen. Parton's account of being embarrassed while shooting take after take of a scene in which Reynolds' character picks her up to carry her over a threshold is wince-inducing. In recalling the experience, she focuses on her own responsibility in the scene, admitting she felt like a failure for her weight.

Parton's impoverished childhood, during which deprivation and hunger helped form her psyche, surely complicated her relationship to the already pained matter of a woman's appetite and body size.

"My daddy and mama, they just think I'm dyin' or somethin'," Parton told Chantal Westerman on a 1987 *Good Morning America* segment soon after she became noticeably thinner (much to the media's obsession). "... At home, my daddy always says, 'if you're gainin' weight, you're a-pickin' up. And if you're losin' weight, you're a-fallin' off.'

So Daddy said, 'Boy, you're a-fallin' off. You're still a-fallin' off, aintcha?'"

When Parton was a child, her infant brother died — possibly due or related to poor nutrition — and her father spent decades farming and working construction to ensure his 11 surviving children didn't starve to death. While Parton has pointed out that she's not underweight for a petite woman, and her "dramatic weight loss" in the '80s was, for her, a shift to feeling more healthy rather than less, a culture and family shaped by the Great Depression and even the European famines their ancestors fled will see shrinking size as potential cause for alarm.

Meanwhile, as Carson and Milsap's quips document, what culture did to reconcile the confounding matter of Dolly Parton — a quick mind, a pretty face, a creative genius, and a huge rack all rolled into one — was to make her the punchline of a joke about big tits.

That joke became so pervasive in the American consciousness that I recall being a child on a playground in the 1980s watching little boys put balls under their shirts and say, "Look, I'm Dolly Parton." Or, "What's this?" they'd ask and turn their hands upside down with just the middle finger extended. (Answer: "Dolly Parton standing behind a tree.")

Parton reclaimed the joke, of course; you'll often find her referencing her own bosom before anyone else has a chance to. She built a career on that sort of spirit. But it was a perilous emotional journey to gain command over the forces that sought to diminish her.

Not long after she "lost the weight" that decade, Parton had breast augmentation surgery, which she has discussed in general terms in her book and elsewhere. Photos from early in her career show that, while her breasts might now be termed "fake," they're about the same size they were when they were

"real." People find the resulting figure — a tiny woman with breasts that don't seem to match her size — shocking. But it's not all that surprising that a woman whose name was made synonymous with breasts might see fit to reclaim not just the joke but the breast size itself — as if to make clear, perhaps, that no punchline had caused her to feel shame.

Parton always smiled and laughed when asked about the hard juxtaposition of her childhood in poverty, her career as a musician and business owner, and her celebrity as a female sex symbol. But such forces take a toll, even on a woman who "made it" because of her natural grit.

It was a painful time for the women who blazed the trail Parton was on — a trail most blocked and treacherous for women of color, gay women, and others outside the cisgender, straight, white mold more palatable to American systems of power. For any woman on that path, the decade was a cluster of mixed messages: Work a "man's job" but for less pay than men. Wear shoulder pads to evoke a man's strength but also high heels to click delicately down the hallway. Be independent enough to drive to the office, but answer to a male boss and cook your husband's dinner when you both get home from work.

That mess of expectations has changed little in the last 30 years, of course, but in the '80s it had a newness that left American culture spinning and drove even tough-as-nails Parton to collapse. Such a woman often pays a severe price, because in her world she is everyone else's support system. Who, then, looks after her?

In the early '80s, Parton experienced her darkest period: a physical and emotional breakdown during which she pondered suicide. Her personal crash happened to coincide with the post-feminism backlash's first big victory — defeat of the Equal Rights Amendment in 1982.

Parton's book names her longtime agent and intimate Sandy Gallin, the legendary talent shepherd who also helmed Michael Jackson's career and who died last April, as offering some nurturing guidance to help her through her severe depression. Ultimately, though, Parton had to do what so many women must in order to find a life that suits them rather than everyone around them: Burn it all down and rebuild.

Around that time, Parton fired some longtime associates, including band members and an accounting firm that kept forgetting that she called the shots with her own money. She also had a partial hysterectomy, she has said without completely outlining the reasons. One positive result she has noted is getting off the estrogen-overdose birth control pills then on the market, but it was also a moment of reckoning about the children she had chosen to forego thus far but now certainly would not have.

After cleaning house in her business, her band, her cupboards, her bloodstream, and even her own womb, Parton rebounded from the emotional collapse. Her thoughts got more positive, her body came into balance, and her business began a crescendo that hasn't stopped since.

She didn't need to kill herself, she wrote in her book, because she'd experienced what some cultures call a shamanic death. "By the grace of God," she writes, "I had [died] without experiencing it in the actual physical sense."

Parton had been actively, consciously evolving since adolescence, every phase an improvement on the last — from a poor country girl to a Nashville hopeful, from Porter Wagoner's micromanaged co-star to crossover solo artist, from small-screen singer to big-screen actress. Now she'd achieved the level of fame and fortune she'd hustled toward all her life, bottomed out emotionally, and found herself the same woman she'd always been, just psychologically reborn. What would be the next goal? She had conquered a man's world the best a woman could, and found it a place that would treat her like shit even when she was on top. There was really only one thing left to do, then: Make her own damn world.

Welcome to Dollywood

"I never got to go to Disneyland as a child, but I was always fascinated with it," Parton told *Maverick* magazine in 2011, almost 20 years after opening her own "world" in the Smoky Mountains. In the 1980s, as a homesick, newly minted movie star disgusted with the Hollywood she dreamed of as a child, Parton went back to the Smokies to create a place called Dollywood.

Dollywood amusement park wouldn't be just a capitalist enterprise, though. It was her vision for energizing her home's ailing rural economy and putting its people to work — including her own family members.

"I knew it would be a great place for all the hardworkin', good-hearted, honest people in this area that don't have jobs," she told *Maverick*. It would be a joyful place, she imagined, full of fun, music, rides, craftsmanship, and culture reflecting her native region.

"A lot of my businesspeople said: 'That's a big mistake, that is a great way to lose all your money,'" Parton told Reuters in 2016. "But I had a feeling in my stomach that it was the right thing to do, so I went ahead with it. Then I got rid of those lawyers and accountants who didn't believe in me, and got new ones who did."

Parton was the boss now, and her business instincts were right. She told Reuters that Dollywood, which celebrated its 30th anniversary in 2016, is the most lucrative investment she ever made. Three million people visit annually. Adding to Parton's home-fried satisfaction, and indeed to the park's success, is that multiple generations of her own kin continue to work and perform at the attraction, as she once envisioned.

Parton's vision for Dollywood's community impact came to fruition, too. Along with two related attractions, the Pigeon Forge, Tennessee, theme park employs about 3,500 people and creates nearly 20,000 jobs in the area, according to an economic study by University of Tennessee researchers this year. Dollywood's economic impact on East Tennessee, according to the researchers, is $1.5 billion. (Yes, that's billion.) Had Parton listened to the people who doubted her business savvy, it's not only she who would have lost out on financial returns, but an entire state.

Not long after Dollywood opened, Parton was approached to host a TV show for ABC. This time it was Parton pooh-poohing someone else's ideas, and for good reason: They sucked. Network television executives forced stupid, awkward skits into *Dolly*, which she had hoped would be a bigger-budget version of the show of the same that she had hosted in Nashville in the 1970s. That earlier show had focused on her natural gifts for music, storytelling, and organic conversation with guests. But ABC insisted, for instance, that each episode of her new show open with her taking a bubble bath on camera. She describes the experience in *My Life:*

I was naïve enough to think that what I wanted would somehow matter to the people in network television. ... There were very few people involved with the show who understood me and what I needed to be doing. Unfortunately, they were not the ones making the decisions. ... I remember sitting in some of those writer/producer meetings and being absolutely amazed. Of the nine or ten men in the room, five had hair transplants, four had some kind of nervous tic, and three had both. ... Sometimes I would hear things brought up and I would wait for everybody to laugh at how ridiculous it was, but the laugh never came. The laugh was on me when the ridiculous idea actually got done.

On *Good Morning America* in 1987, when co-host Charlie Gibson interviewed her about her new show's struggling ratings, Parton defended herself and her hopes for the show.

"We're just kind of weedin' out what ain't workin' really well, which is mostly things I didn't think would work to start with," Parton told Gibson. "Everybody's just trying a little too hard, I think. The bubble bath scene may not show on the show. ... The people don't know what to make of it. 'Why are you taking a bubble bath on television?' I asked that myself. But anyway, you do what you gotta do."

Dignified newsman Gibson's non sequitur in response: "The hair may be false, but everything else is real, right?"

In the segment, Gibson never offered a chance for her to plug her work. So, after he cued her farewell, instead of saying goodbye, Parton listed her upcoming show's guests: Patti LaBelle and others.

"Not to run through the whole cast or anything," Gibson condescended. "Thanks very —"

"Well, I might as well — that's what I'm on television for," Parton interrupted with an incredulous smile and raised eyebrows. "You didn't think I got up just to say hello to you, did ya?"

"Absolutely that's what I thought,"

Gibson shot back with a similarly tense smile, and Parton talked over him again.

"I got up to advertise," she said.

That same year, in a rare occurrence of a member of the press discussing Parton's wit rather than her body, *Washington Post* reporter Jacqueline Trescott incorporated another Parton exchange into a story about new-hire Gibson's flat presence next to *Good Morning America* co-host Joan Lunden.

"Some show business pros are quicker than he is," wrote Trescott. "When he asked entertainer Parton if she had tested the water slide at her theme park, Dollywood, she said, 'It's no kind of ride for a woman with a hairdo like mine.' Gibson gamely moved on to her successful diet and asked her waistline measurement. Parton replied, 'Between 18 and 23. People think I am big busted but it is because I squish it all in.' Then he asked her about her lucrative contract with ABC to produce a series of variety shows and she replied, 'It takes a lot of money to make a person look this cheap.'

"Swallowing his comebacks, as the control room collapsed in convulsions, Gibson signed off, 'Thanks ever so much.'"

Parton got the last laugh about her TV show, too. Thanks to a well-negotiated contract, ABC had to pay her millions to cancel the show when it tanked. She walked away, too, with a deepened wisdom about the business world, which — in a rare instance of overriding her natural diplomacy and going for the throat — she outlines at length in *My Life:*

Don't assume that the people on the inside know what they're doing. He may have a big office and a fancy suit. He may have the power to hire you or not. But he probably has no idea whether or not you have any talent. Even if he has an opinion, he probably has to clear it with guys in even bigger offices with even more expensive suits (and even less of a clue).

... Although the ratio may be better than in some other businesses, show business is still essentially a man's world. As a woman, that can be difficult to deal with. Especially if you are a five-foot-two blonde with a hick accent. In addition, the difficulty factor is multiplied by two for every cup size. In short, being a woman in show business is like being a bird dog in heat. If you stand still, they'll screw you. If you run, they'll bite you in the ass ...

There are basically two kinds of men you have to deal with in business: the ones who want to screw you out of money, and the ones who want to screw you, period. The second guy is the easiest to deal with. If I catch a man who is not looking into my eyes as he talks to me, I have scored two really big points with him already. A smart woman can take a man who thinks with his small head and quickly turn the would-be screwer into the screwee.

I should point out that I am not interested in screwing anybody [professionally]. I never want anything more than what's fair. The problem is, I never want anything less either. In the old-boy school of business, if a woman walks away from the table with what's rightfully hers, the man feels screwed anyway. I have to admit that adds to the satisfaction of making a fair deal. 'How was it for you, old boy?'"

As the '80s waned, Parton was in full bloom as the icon we know today: a switch-smart business shark with a physical presentation society might read as hyper-sexualized but that is curated for her own delight. What man did she need to turn by that point anyway? She was on the back side of 40 and had long been the boss.

Her 1989 music video for "Why'd You Come in Here Lookin' Like That," from her classic album *White Limozeen*, is a cheesy but delightfully meta staging of auditions for the male lead in a music video. She didn't happen to write that number-one hit, which laments how fine a bad boy's ass looks in "painted-on jeans" and which she still performs with conviction at age 71. But in the video, she's in charge, watching from a dark theater seat with the house lights down as men walk on stage, flex their muscles, and represent caricatures of various sorts of jerks. She laughs and loves them anyway. ("I think they're all real sweet," she tells the casting director when he asks for her thoughts.) Her reward for her Christian patience: A perfectly chiseled janitor in cowboy boots and a cut-off denim shirt accidentally walks into the spotlight with a push broom. Perhaps in answer to Charlie Gibson, Johnny Carson, Ronnie Milsap, and all the powerful, famous men who ignored her artistry in favor of discussing her body, Parton looks the janitor up and down as if to say, "You're hired."

Media Scrutiny

In 1983, when Parton visited the UK for a TV special called *Dolly in London*, a male reporter at a press conference asked her if it were true that she didn't consider herself a sex symbol. She explained that she dressed the way she did not as a gimmick to turn on her fans but because she was "impressed with the people back home" — a reference to "trashy" women whose makeup and hair dye she coveted in a rural community where few women had access to such things due to both poverty and religious code. She enjoyed reveling in the picture she could now afford to paint.

"I feel sexy," Parton said. "I like being a woman. If I'd-a been a man, I'd-a probably been a drag queen."

Two questions later, after a lighthearted reference to *Best Little Whorehouse* and rounds of laughter, a female journalist solemnly asked for Parton's opinion on prostitution. The crowd of journalists gasped, apparently sensing something untoward about the question or its timing. Parton's smile fell a little, and she took a second to gather her response for a question she clearly didn't relish answering.

"Oh, I close the whorehouse down," Parton said to laughs before turning serious. "I love everybody. ... And, like I say, who am I to judge? I got enough problems of my own." Parton paused for a beat, but the room remained silent. She turned back to the questioner, as if to make sure she would have to squirm too. "Are you a prostitute?" The woman looked down, embarrassed.

For Parton, the old boys came in many forms: Hollywood directors, Nashville producers, media interviewers. As evidenced from that journalist with the prostitute question, though, Parton's exchanges with the era's female journalists were often just as problematic as Gibson's patronizing or Carson's creepy comments.

In 1977 on *The Barbara Walters Special*, Walters caught up with Parton playing a rodeo in Kansas City — the sort of gig her considerable stardom had not quite yet outgrown. Walters interviewed Parton, then 31 and beginning her pop music crossover, on the tour bus she shared with her band. Over the course of the conversation, Walters asked her if any "hanky panky" went on amid Parton and her band; whether she hit puberty at a young age; whether her breasts were real; why she wore the trashy wigs and makeup; how she could possibly keep a husband if she was always on the road.

(Parton: "I've got better things to do than to sit around in my room thinkin', 'Oh, what's Carl doin' tonight?'")

At one point, Walters asked Parton to stand up.

"I want people to see — you know," Walters said as she drew an hourglass with her hands.

"I'm not all that curvy in this outfit," Parton said as she stood up to oblige.

"Oh, it's not bad," Walters said, looking over at the camera crew to make sure they were getting the shot while Parton put her hands on her hips and endured the stunt. "Do you give your measurements?"

"No," Parton said. "I always just say I weigh a hundred and twenty."

Eventually Parton felt compelled to point out that she was a human being.

"I'm very real where it counts ... and that's inside — as far as my outlook on life and the way I care about people and the way I care about myself," Parton said. "Show business is a money-making joke."

"But do you ever feel that you're a joke," Walters said, her cadence making a statement rather than a question. "That people make fun of you."

"Oh, I know they make fun of me," Parton said. "All these years people has [sic] thought the joke was on me, but it's actually been on the public. I know exactly what I'm doing, and I can change it any time."

Parton went on to explain that her deep security — in her talent, in her good heart, in all the things Walters didn't ask her about — was precisely why she could "piddle around" with makeup and clothes in a manner in which she, not society and its would-be approval, was in command.

The interview may be disturbing in hindsight, but it was par for the course at the time — the contrast an encouraging reminder that we have, at least in the matter of media treatment, come far. While women still get sexist questions, most of today's leading talk-show hosts wouldn't treat Parton with such plain disrespect, and if they did an army of pissed off tweets would be hot on their heels.

Socioeconomic class is a different matter, even slower than race or gender to arise in America's self-awareness. Walters asked about Parton's childhood, and Parton offered an earnest answer about the log cabin, the Little Pigeon River, the many children. Walters then

interjected with a tone that I recognize well: the upper-middle-class or affluent woman diminishing a "poor" woman's origins.

"Dolly, where I come from, would I have called you a hillbilly?"

Parton smiled. "If you had of, it would have been something very natural, but I would have probably kicked your shins or something." Parton laughed, Walters didn't.

"But when I think of hillbillies, am I thinking of your kind of people?" Walters continued.

This, I'm afraid, is the sort of exchange that women from particular origins experience today. Parton was, it often seems, a trailblazer among trailblazers, miles ahead of the day's avowed feminists while being chastised by them for both her tight clothes and her progressive approach to marriage.

Even sympathetic interviewers such as Oprah Winfrey, with whom Parton had an obvious mutual affection and respect, fixated on Parton as an object; on her talk show in the late-'80s, Winfrey had Parton stand up for the audience to examine her not once but twice.

The third pillar of the late-20th-century talk show trinity, alongside Walters and Winfrey, added a male perspective to the sexist gauntlet.

"I know guys who wouldn't let you out of the house," Phil Donahue told Parton during a taping in the mid-'80s. Parton laughed and assured that her longtime husband wasn't possessive. An audience member then wanted to know whether her husband had helped her in her career. He preferred to stay out of her business affairs and its show-business trappings, Parton explained.

"That's hard to believe he could be so removed from your professional life," Donahue replied.

Parton offered a thoughtful response, and suddenly Donahue was next to the stage reaching his hand toward her. He had stopped listening and was on to the next thing — you guessed it.

"You won't mind if I ask you to just stand up for just one second," Donahue said, ushering her up onto her feet.

Donahue and Winfrey both asked Parton to address her childlessness. By then she was past the age of 40, the question having shifted from "will you" to "why didn't you."

"That's by choice, isn't it?" Donahue asked.

"No, actually I can't have children,"

Parton replied, offering the same line she gave Winfrey about "female problems." The truth, Parton has admitted in recent years, was more complicated; she sometimes imagined having children but was pleased to continue focusing solely on her career, a preference so unacceptable for a woman of child-bearing age at the time that she sometimes circled around the direct truth when answering the question over the years.

These talk-show time capsules, which say more about the cultural moment and network ratings expectations than about the interviewers, amount to a thorough compilation of all the questions successful women — from celebrities to politicians to any woman with a career in the public eye — receive and men don't, overlaid with a sense of awe in Parton's presence that is at once admiration and objectification.

On television, Parton at least had the opportunity to respond in real time and hope the producers would edit the tape in a fair manner. Print was a much more dicey prospect: chatting with a writer, most often a man, for him to go off and write what he pleased.

In one particularly barf-worthy *Rolling Stone* story, penned in 1977 by Chet Flippo, the longtime pre-eminent music writer in the country arena, Flippo unfurls a middle-aged man's meta-gonzo fantasy about the time he spent with Parton for the story. She rides next to him in a convertible, him imagining the encounter as a date — he should have made dinner reservations, he told her. He was sure to reference that a couple conversations were in her motel room, though that was standard protocol for stars doing press on the road. He ended on a quote about Parton newly sprouting breasts as a child and the other children tearing at her jacket to see underneath, and by then a reader wonders whether he's just making shit up; magazine journalists at the time weren't known for their meticulous notes. Flippo wasn't just some sleazy hack, it should be pointed out. He was beloved as a fixture in music journalism. But around Parton — an extreme embodiment of what men have rendered pornographic — decent people often found themselves flailing.

What do you do if you're Dolly Parton and subjected to these absurd sorts of celebrity interviews for decades? You take a movie role that allows you to play the broadcasting host. In 1992's

Straight Talk, alongside James Woods' investigative newspaper reporter, Parton's character is a well-intentioned radio talk show host who doesn't know what she's doing and is secretly actually a clinical psychologist.

Parton noted in *My Life* that, unlike some of her other film experiences, she loved making *Straight Talk*, in large part because director Barnett Kellman "was willing to share what he knew with me" and "had a nice way of doing it." Her natural wit was allowed to shine, her on-set countryisms often making it into the script in a way that exalted rather than lampooned "homespun" language. Just as she had previously set a male boss straight in *Nine to Five*, reclaimed the joke about her breasts, and turned the word "Hollywood" into "Dollywood," she flipped the script and put herself in the interviewer's chair with *Straight Talk*.

The Freedom to Work

Parton started the 1980s with her first movie role, Doralee in *Nine to Five*, and ended the decade with what might be her most beloved one: Truvy, the sweet-and-sassy beauty shop owner in 1989's *Steel Magnolias*.

She recalled in *My Life* that director Herbert Ross "didn't particularly like me or Julia Roberts at the start and [he] was very hard on her. ... He told me I couldn't act." A generation of women would disagree. At a spring 2017 screening of the quintessential tearjerker in Austin, tickets came with a tiny faux hairspray bottle that movie-theater employees had labeled with "Truvy's," and the mostly female audience cheered when the character came onscreen.

Earlier this year, in a *Garden & Gun* spread reflecting on the beloved film about Southern women, co-star Shirley MacLaine remembered Parton as a heroically easygoing presence in spite of the stresses on set.

"It was really hot," MacLaine said. "There was Dolly with a waist cincher no more than 16 inches around and heels about two feet high and a wig that must have weighed 23 pounds. And she's the only one who didn't sweat. She never complained about anything. Never. The rest of us were always complaining."

Screenwriter Robert Harling remembered Parton the same way.

"We were shooting part of the Christmas scene, and this was in the dead of August, and we were sitting out on the porch of Truvy's beauty shop," Harling said. "We were waiting, and there was a lot of stop and start. The women were dressed for Christmas, and Dolly was sitting on the swing. She had on that white cashmere sweater with the marabou around the neck, and she was just swinging, cool as a cucumber. Julia said, 'Dolly, we're dying and you never say a word. Why don't you let loose?' Dolly very serenely smiled and said, 'When I was young and had nothing, I wanted to be rich and famous, and now I am. So I'm not going to complain about anything.' "

You can bet that's why she's never complained about the mistreatments I've outlined here. Parton is smart enough to teach the applicable lessons when she gets the chance, though. When *Cineaste* magazine asked her in 1990 what she'd discovered in making *Steel Magnolias*, Parton didn't say "that male bosses are still assholes ten years after *Nine to Five*." She instead defended one of her castmates.

"Daryl Hannah was the big surprise to me. She's beautiful and sweet as anything, but lord, what an actress," Parton said. "... I had no idea what a great talent that girl had, 'cause I'd always thought of her as the pretty, long-legged blonde, y'know, getting my head into the same kind of stereotyped thinkin' that annoys me when it happens to me. Daryl takes her acting very seriously and has a curious intelligence and intuition about her. Rare."

In this way, Parton was the skillful, "uneducated" ambassador of the messages middle- and upper-class women discussed among themselves but could not impart to the masses from the often-rarefied spaces of college campuses and activist circles. Most women I grew up among in rural Kansas do not know who Gloria Steinem is, but they know the lines in Parton's late-20th century movies by heart and recognize themselves in her image.

Steinem wrote books about reproductive rights, the patriarchal institution of marriage, and the socioeconomic inequality that often accompanies motherhood, for instance, and Parton gave *Maclean's* the same message in 2014: "One of the reasons I think I've done so well is because I've had the freedom to work," Parton said. "I never had children and I never had a husband who's wanted to bitch about everything I did."

In one of the more improbable photographs from my childhood, a yellowed square with rounded corners developed around 1984, I'm about four years old and wearing a white tank top printed with the *Ms.* magazine logo. The tiny kids' shirt must have been bought at a garage sale; no one in my family subscribed to *Ms.*, and I'd never even heard of Gloria Steinem's seminal periodical until I was a college-educated adult. But there I am, in rural Kansas, where no one used the word "feminism" in the 1980s, wearing a piece of feminist apparel — not because my mom wanted to make a statement but because it was on the five-cents card table on someone's Wichita driveway.

I tweeted the photo before seeing Steinem speak a few weeks before the 2016 presidential election: "Seeing @GloriaSteinem tonight! No feminism talk in 1980s rural KS, but Mom embodied it — & got me this at a yard sale." Whoever runs Steinem's account "liked" my tweet, which I noted was one of her mere 15 or so such "likes" at the time — that small, silly transference perhaps my most treasured encounter with a hero.

To have my mother's strength as a woman in the world — raised in abuse and poverty, 17 when she became pregnant with me, tenacious as a worker in order to pay the bills, intellectually and creatively gifted but without the chance to go to college, physically beautiful to such an extent she was coveted as an object the second she entered a room — validated by Steinem or someone representing her was for me a union of my bifurcated socioeconomic experience as a woman in the world.

That evening at Steinem's talk on the University of Texas campus, I was struck by her explanation for why, how in the world, such venomous misogyny could overrun a presidential election in 2016. The moment a woman is statistically most likely to be murdered by her male abuser, Steinem pointed out, is when she escapes. Losing control of her is the unbearable threat that makes the violent ex-husband snap.

Expanding this idea to a patriarchy losing control of a hundred million women would indeed explain a lot at the societal level that would appear to be a regression since the gains of the late 20th century: Abortion provider George Tiller's murder in Wichita in 2009, Clinton's treatment — and subsequent loss — in 2016, the reliable track record of violence against and hatred toward women among male perpetrators of this century's mass-shooting epidemic. It would explain too, perhaps, why Parton was turned into a boob joke around the time she became her own boss and conquered show business.

Like Steinem, Parton is an icon of American womanhood in the 20th century, still going full-force today, perhaps with the energy other women their age who made more orthodox decisions must offer to their grandchildren. Steinem is no daughter of privilege, but the two women nonetheless had different experiences of socioeconomic class: one went to college, and one took a guitar to Nashville. In different ways and with different tacks, they both paved the road that allowed us to at least nominate a woman for president in 2016. It is that same road that women of Generation X and beyond walk — at least one of them, I bet, not just to be nominated but to win.

When that woman eventually becomes president, she will face the same sexist media questions that women like Dolly Parton and Hillary Clinton have faced, and she will be criticized for her appearance and attendant decisions as both of them have been. She will remember when men held some sort of power she was forced to navigate, whether the harassment Doralee endured for a paycheck, the body-shaming Parton received in Hollywood, or the second-guessing she received from accountants on her own payroll. But she will be this country's first female boss, her leadership inevitably shaped by the trials of womanhood.

In *Nine to Five*, the triumphant female employees restructure the entire office while their boss is collared and chained in his own bedroom — a veritable justice spree of overdue raises and recognition for cubicles full of women and some productivity-enhancing redecorating to boot.

So that some female might have such a chance to improve this ailing democracy, we must give women the freedom to do feminism however they please, whether it strikes us as correct or not. Leading feminists shaming women for campaigning for Democratic socialist Bernie Sanders when he opposed Clinton in the 2016 primaries is not all that different from Barbara Walters criticizing Parton's style choices in 1977.

If Parton's struggles and successes as an implicit rather than explicit feminist teach us anything, it's that the most authentic female power does not always align with the politics of a movement. If you take Parton's decisions 30 years ago and hold them up against some of the things said and written by activists, academics, and other movement-approved experts from the same time, I would wager that Parton's feminism has aged just as well and in some cases far better.

Lucky for all of us, there is a generation of women coming into power that benefited from both, whether directly or indirectly. They didn't all get to go to college, but they are all the daughters of *Nine to Five* — the children against whose lives one can map Parton's metamorphosis from country star to global icon to business empress. They are old enough to be divorced but young enough to still get asked whether they'll finally have a baby; old enough to remember record players in every house but young enough to have been shaped by hip-hop. They watched their mothers be patronized and mistreated so that some future generation might not have to be, and they are equipped to undo the gains made by anti-feminist backlashes over the course of their lifetimes. Today, they are the three women fed up at the office, ready to join forces and hog-tie the male boss until they get some goddamn respect.

Some people might describe *Nine to Five* as a revenge fantasy, but I think of it as a parable about justice. It isn't their boss's suffering they want but their own fair treatment — a request that could only be misconstrued as misandry in the eyes of male privilege.

During Parton's hugely successful 2016 tour for her latest album, *Pure and Simple*, between song performances, she offered a running commentary

to make sure everyone knew who was cutting the checks. She objectified the hot male cowboy who brought out her instruments: "He's handsome, ain't he, girls? He's purdy, ain't he, boys? ... You know that old saying: Make yourself useful and ornamental."

And she told the story about why there was a drum machine on stage: The drummer slated to join the tour, she said, had frowned at her costumes for the show. It was supposed to be a simple, stripped-down production evoking a front porch in Tennessee rather than a Vegas megashow, and here was Dolly with her usual rhinestones and big hair and heels. She should make her wardrobe more plain too, he told her.

If the story is true — in the tradition of rural storytelling, Parton has a way of carving the details to suit her intended punchline — giving Parton advice about her stage appearance took some real brass. Parton might have worked for male directors in Hollywood along the way, but she has been in charge of her own music productions since leaving *The Porter Wagoner Show* 30 years ago. In *Dolly: My Life and Other Unfinished Business*, she included a black-and-white photo of Wagoner ceremoniously presenting her 20-something self with a piece of precious jewelry; young Parton wears a beehive wig and a tight, dutiful smile. The caption reads, "Me and Porter: Oh boy, a ring, but what I wanted was a raise."

In the end, Parton didn't just get a raise — she got the whole world, and the drummer she employed for this tour apparently hadn't heard. She told him the two words every woman should at least have the chance to say: "You're fired." And that's why there was a drum machine instead of a man hitting drums. "I left him in Nashville. I saved a lot of money," Parton said, gesturing affectionately toward the drum machine. "And it don't talk back." ■

> What culture did to reconcile the confounding matter of Dolly Parton — a quick mind, a pretty face, a creative genius, and a huge rack all rolled into one — was to make her the punchline of a joke about big tits.

Contributors

ALEXA PETERS is a freelance writer living in the beautiful Pacific Northwest. A graduate of Western Washington University, she loves to write about the things she's most passionate about: music, writing, travel, social justice, feminism, and self-help. She's written for a wide array of publication including *The Seattle Times*, Amy Poehler's Smart Girls, *Paste, Seattle, Seattle Weekly*, and now *No Depression*.

ALLISON HUSSEY is a North Carolina native whose favorite things include record shopping, critters, biscuits, folklore, and social justice. She now lives in Durham and is the music editor at *INDY Week*, with other work appearing at *Pitchfork*, Bandcamp, *Noisey,* and The Bluegrass Situation.

CAMERON MATTHEWS is a writer, editor, and musician based in New York City. He previously managed editorial operations for The Bluegrass Situation and was the web editor for NoDepression.com.

CAITLIN CARY is delighted and gratified to have come "full circle." She appeared on *No Depression's* cover as a member of her band Whiskeytown in the '90s and provided artwork for the cover of this issue, paying homage to her one of her hometown idols, Elizabeth Cotten. Cary devotes the bulk of her time to visual art, a form of fabric collage for which she coined the term "Needle Print," and she maintains an open studio in Raleigh's Artspace. She plays shows now and again with her bands Tres Chicas and The Small Ponds, and she'd welcome a visit any time you find yourself in Raleigh.

CORBIE HILL is a freelance writer who lives on three wooded acres in Pittsboro, North Carolina, with his wife and two daughters. His work appears in the *News & Observer, INDY Week*, and a handful of other papers and magazines, though if he had it all to do over again he'd be a scientist.

DREW CHRISTIE is a Seattle-based animator and illustrator. His work has been featured by *The New York Times, Huffington Post, The Atlantic,* and others.

HENRY CARRIGAN writes a weekly column about music books for nodepression.com and is sales and marketing manager for *No Depression* in print. He also writes about music and books for *Living Blues, Downbeat, Publishers Weekly,* and *BookPage.*

HOWARD RAINS is an artist and fiddler obsessed with painting and playing an archaic style of fiddling from his home state of Texas. He enjoys traveling and performing with his wife and musical partner.

JENNY RITTER is a West Coast Canadian indie-folk musician/rock choir director who loves doing illustration on the side.

JONATHAN BERNSTEIN is a writer and fact-checker living in Brooklyn. His work has been published in the *Oxford American, The Guardian, Rolling Stone, Pitchfork,* and *American Songwriter.*

JUSTIN JOFFE is a Brooklyn-based journalist covering music, art, media, and technology. He has written for numerous publications, including *Spin, Noisey, Relix,* and *Flaunt.* He's a full-time contributor to *Observer's* arts section.

KAIA KATER is a singer-songwriter who was born of Afro-Caribbean descent in Quebec. She grew up with deep ties to Canadian folk music in her Toronto home and studied Appalachian music in West Virginia. Her latest album, *Nine Pin* (2016), casts an unflinching eye at the realities faced every day by people of color in North America.

KIM RUEHL is a recovering songwriter who unexpectedly landed in a job as a music writer in 2005. Since then, her work has been published in *Billboard, Yes, Seattle Weekly,* NPR, and elsewhere. She's the editor-in-chief of *No Depression* and, these days, uses her songwriting skills to improv showtunes for her three-year-old daughter. She lives in Asheville, North Carolina, with her family.

LEE ZIMMERMAN has been a freelance writer for publications like *American Songwriter, Blurt,* and *Billboard* for 20 years. He lives in Maryville, Tennessee, with his wife.

MIKE SEELY is a freelance writer and former editor of *Seattle Weekly*. He lives in Seattle, Washington.

SARAH SMARSH is a journalist who writes about socioeconomic class in America. She has reported on public policy for *Harper's*, NewYorker.com, *The Guardian, Guernica,* and others. Her essays on cultural boundaries have been published by *Aeon, McSweeney's,* and more. She formerly reviewed female country acts for alt-weeklies in the Midwest. Smarsh's book on the working poor and her upbringing in rural Kansas is forthcoming from Scribner. She lives in Kansas and Texas.

STEPHEN DEUSNER is a Tennessee native now living in Bloomington, Indiana. His work appears regularly in *Pitchfork, American Songwriter, Uncut,* the Bluegrass Situation, Stereogum, Salon, and elsewhere.

RIGHTEOUS BABE RECORDS

Ani DiFranco

NO DEPRESSION

Winter 2017: Singer-Songwriters

It always starts with the song. Where the song comes from might be different depending on the writer. But that compelling urge to pair lyrics and melody, grand ideas and tiny moments, tied together with rhythm and music, is what motivates and inspires the songwriter. How it happens is often hard to put into words, but for the winter issue of *No Depression*, we've spoken to some of the finest singer-songwriters around to explore the craft of songs.

Including:

Josh Ritter / Ani DiFranco / Jackson Browne / Chris Hillman / The Avett Brothers / Sam Beam / Daniel Lanois / Lori McKenna / Jolie Holland & Sam Parton / Allison Moorer & Shelby Lynne / Larry Campbell & Teresa Williams / Susan Werner / Samantha Crain / Inside songwriting retreats / Essays by Janis Ian and Wild Ponies, and more.

Cover art by Jessica Husband
Paintings by Dan Bern
Photography by Rose Cousins

Spring 2018: Appalachia

Explore the past, present, and future of this deeply musical part of the country. Old Crow Medicine Show's Ketch Secor writes about the region's rich influence. We also talk about Kentucky with Ben Sollee, and explore the jazz, funk, and old-time scenes of Asheville, North Carolina, and beyond.

Part of the FreshGrass Foundation

No Depression is brought to you by the FreshGrass Foundation, a 501(c)(3) nonprofit organization dedicated to preserving and promoting the past, present, and future of American roots music. In addition to publishing *No Depression* and presenting the annual FreshGrass Festival at Mass MoCA in Western Massachusetts each September, the Foundation funds cash awards for up-and-coming musicians, the *No Depression* Singer-Songwriter Award, the *No Depression* Writing Fellow, and more. Visit freshgrass.org for more information

NODEPRESSION.COM/SUBSCRIBE

Screen Door

WHY TELL THE STORIES OF OUR FOREMOTHERS?

BY KAIA KATER

In her autobiography, *I Put a Spell On You*, the great jazz artist Nina Simone wrote of playing live shows as a bullfight, and herself as the toreador. "I had the ability to make people feel on a deep level," she wrote. "It's difficult to describe because it's not something you can analyze — to get near what [the music is] about you have to play it."

As a musician, I know this to be true. I also know that the desire to make one's mark on the world is deeply human. I've attempted to decipher landscapes of songs other people wrote, but somehow this feels cheap. The relentless attempt to explain away the beauty behind any piece of art is akin to the curious nipper who strips off the bark from the tree just to know what lies beneath. Often I find that the deeper I mine into songs — those I've written and those by others — the less I know. This is both a comforting and terrifying notion.

My favorite songwriters are those who frighten me. Who guide me to the darkest star of the heart and have me gaze at its many moons with animistic curiosity.

I look to heroes like Ola Belle Reed and Elizabeth Cotten, who were both determined to be heard. Or like my own great-grandmother, who taught herself to read and write in secret while working for white families. Her story is not special. It is the reality of women living as servants in colonial lands. They lie muted in the grave, and we go on in soundless remembrance.

But songs are the noise. They are the all-encompassing dialectic reflection of life. The songwriter is the poet, who swims to deep waters and returns with tales to tell. Who comforts without comforting.

Yet for women in music to claim

their own space as poets comes with the challenge of fending off those who want to take that space away. Female musicians have been called divas, vamps, songbirds. They are pronounced to be coquettish, waiflike, serpentine, tremulous, and turgid — everything but genius, prolific, or prodigal.

During an interview with *Maclean*'s magazine in 2014, Joni Mitchell spoke plainly of her decision to compose: "It's a man's world. Men wrote most of the songs for women and they were mostly tales of seduction. I wrote my own songs. That ended that." Mitchell's simple dissection of 150 years of recorded music was sobering. Why is it considered such a revolutionary act for a woman to write her own songs?

Music writer Alexandra Pollard bridges the gap to this question. In her article "Why Are Only Women Described as 'Confessional' Singer Songwriters?", Pollard suggests that

while women are presumed to be more emotionally sensitive than men, they have also historically operated within the private, domestic sphere. As such, Pollard affirms, they have had to work harder to externalize their thoughts in order to prove them worthy of public consumption. Thus, women's words — and by extension, their songs — are largely considered to be worth less than men's in the consumption of art. This results in unrelenting frustration when, for example, the great songwriter Kathleen Brennan is referred to simply as Tom Waits' wife — as was the case in a 2016 *Boston Herald* headline: "Tom Waits, his wife, John Prine receive songwriting awards." Or when, as Canadian pop artist Grimes points out, the basic desire for human equality is met with rampant hostility and the accusation of abject hatred for men.

This couldn't be further from the truth. The truth, though maybe it's not said so much anymore, is that playing music out in the world feels like opening a portal that no one else gets a chance to pass through.

I became a songwriter mostly because I knew it could be done. It wasn't so frightening anymore. I feel like I skipped the line to the tilt-a-whirl and went straight to the front. And now I am tasked with creating landscapes and inviting crowds of strangers to step into them. The possibility of failure, of rejection, of a missed connection, is what makes it exciting. As Joni Mitchell put it to Joe Smith in 1986: "You can give me audience of 40,000 hostile people and I won't even break a sweat. You give me a room of 200 adoring people and my mouth will dry up."

Sometimes I am asked how I could possibly seek to make a living with roots music. On bad nights, I ask myself these needling questions too. The plain conclusion I have come to is that we belong to something larger than any one of us. The world is chaos, and songs are a brief acknowledgment of that chaos. We split the atom in our own way, note by note and song by song.

Thus, the importance of telling the stories of women in music has always been about taking up the space that these stories deserve. It's about writing them so that someone down the line will read them. It's about leaving them in ink somewhere on this spinning pale blue dot.